Investigating STEM With Infants and Toddlers (Birth–3)

Investigating STEM With Infants and Toddlers (Birth–3)

EDITED BY

Beth Dykstra Van Meeteren and Sherri Peterson,
with Rosemary Geiken, Jill Uhlenberg, and Sonia Yoshizawa

STEM for Our Youngest Learners Series

TEACHERS COLLEGE PRESS

TEACHERS COLLEGE | COLUMBIA UNIVERSITY
NEW YORK AND LONDON

Published by Teachers College Press,® 1234 Amsterdam Avenue, New York, NY 10027

Front cover photo by Sherri Peterson.

Library of Congress Cataloging-in-Publication Data is available at loc.gov

ISBN 978-0-8077-6694-1 (paper)
ISBN 978-0-8077-6695-8 (hardcover)
ISBN 978-0-8077-8102-9 (ebook)

Printed on acid-free paper
Manufactured in the United States of America

Contents

List of Figures

List of Photographs

List of Photographs

Preface

The purpose of this book is to provide a resource for infant and toddler educators who wish to implement STEM experiences in their settings. It is a practical guide, written in a style that is accessible to educators from a wide range of educational backgrounds and experiences. The focus of the book is to describe our view of how infants and toddlers learn through an inquiry process when supported by adults who are passionate about this age group.

The authors have many years of experience, both in preparing early childhood educators to work with infants and toddlers and in working with the birth–3 age group. We recognize the need for high-quality curriculum for this age group and address that need through a focus on the most effective approach to offering that curriculum.

The book is written in two parts. In Part I, the first three chapters provide a foundation in thinking about inquiry learning and teaching, how the environment can support children's learning, and supportive components for educators, such as observation, assessment, and documentation. In Part II, the remaining six chapters cover STEM topics that the authors have explored with infants and toddlers. These chapters include a rationale for offering these topics, vignettes and photos of children exploring the topics, and examples of how educators have supported infants and toddlers in their learning. We describe situations when children have used materials in both expected and unexpected ways.

Chapter 1 includes our view of inquiry learning and teaching. We introduce the Infant Toddler Inquiry Learning Model (ITILM) to help the reader understand what inquiry learning looks like in these very young children. We also introduce inquiry from the educator's perspective through the Inquiry Teaching Model (ITM) to demonstrate how educators can initiate and respond to young children's explorations.

Chapter 2 discusses the importance of the environment, or environments, because there are multiple facets to an infant and toddler environment, starting with the physical design of space. The social relationships of the environment are included in this chapter, including educator–child relationships and relationships between adults in the space. In addition, we introduce the idea of a promotional or invitational environment that describes how educators support children's learning and development through the environment. The intellectual environment is described through the lens of the ITILM within STEM experiences for infants and toddlers.

Chapter 3 expands the role of adults in teaching through inquiry. This includes educator planning, observing, and assessing learning, and the importance of reflective practice. We examine some assessment strategies that are appropriate for infant or toddler educators, and we also describe the value of observation and documentation of the children's learning, including children with special needs.

These first chapters are foundational to the idea of inquiry learning and teaching. Educators may choose to read the remaining chapters separately, over time, as they begin to try out these STEM experiences in their own classrooms.

Throughout this book we include photos of children exploring materials as well as vignettes of young children from our own classroom experiences, and we analyze these experiences using the ITILM as an organizer. We also include examples within each vignette analysis of how educators have responded to children's actions with supportive comments and encouragement. Using the ITM as an organizer, we discuss three parts of the educator's approach to teaching through inquiry: engaging the learner, providing opportunities, and making decisions.

Chapter 4 describes explorations of water in a variety of containers, including a sensory table or tub. Children explore ideas about water's physical characteristics, beginning ideas about volume, and concepts of water movement. Even these very young children have previous experiences with water, in routine activities during the day, at home, or in sensory table activities. The experiences in this chapter demonstrate the complexity of water as it provides opportunities for children to think about water and its interaction with materials in different ways.

Chapter 5 describes our work with Contents and Containers (C&C). This STEM focus area expands on the water chapter, as the focus allows children to explore a wide variety of plastic containers and other typical items found in most kitchens, some with lids and some without. Contents for the explorations are typical materials found in infant and toddler settings, as well as being safe objects that prove interesting to explore. We include a selection of simple contents, including scarves, fabric balls, nesting boxes and cups, and other plastic toys, found in typical infant or toddler classrooms. This chapter also includes a description of the outcomes we observed, especially in spatial understanding, which is part of mathematics.

Chapter 6 uses variations on the C&C work described in Chapter 5. Chapter 6 is about Chutes and Silos, our approach to inviting children's actions on tubes and balls of various sizes, as well as other materials. Children responded somewhat differently to these materials by exploring both spatial understanding and problem solving. Children clearly explored the ideas of containment inside the tubes, as well as spatial relationships through the sizes and quantity of balls or other objects.

Chapter 7 is about blocks. Many toddler rooms and most infant rooms do not have sets of blocks. Wooden unit block sets rarely are found in classrooms for these very young children. If possible, we recommend making unit blocks available. However, they are expensive, and other kinds of blocks can provide opportunities for exploring space, balance, and creative construction while young children develop ideas about engineering and spatial understanding.

Two final chapters explore other STEM areas. Chapter 8 describes how infants and toddlers can engage with light and shadow. This chapter examines young children's fascination with flashlights or other safe light sources, as well as objects that cast shadows, including the children themselves.

Chapter 9 provides an exploration of sound, a topic that focuses on children's auditory skills, and describes how they can engage in opportunities to distinguish, create, and vary sound. Children are regarded as problem-solvers and engineers while they develop sound concepts such as loud or soft, long or short, high or low, and same or different. Both Chapters 8 and 9 are examples of how initial explorations provide a foundation for later school learning of STEM concepts.

Throughout the book, we include ideas about working with children with special needs of various kinds. Within the birth–3 age group, children with disabilities often are not yet identified. The variety of materials and engagements described in this book provide an approach for adults to include all children in the exploration of STEM topics.

Acknowledgments

We are grateful to the many children, families, and educators who have allowed us to share their learning stories and the photos that illustrate these stories. Without the assistance of these important people, we could not have accomplished our mission of documenting our own understanding about how infants and toddlers learn about the world. We want to give a special thank you to the amazing educators we have had the privilege of working with at the Child Development Center on the campus of the University of Northern Iowa (UNI). These educators opened their classroom doors to collaborate with us as we observed, documented, and reflected on the meaning of children's actions. We hope they found it as meaningful as we did. Our gratitude goes also to the educators working at the Center of Excellence in Early Childhood Learning and Development on the campus of East Tennessee State University.

We would like to thank the early childhood faculty in the College of Education at UNI and the Campus Advisory Committee of the Iowa Regents' Center for Early Developmental Education. The partnerships created have been invaluable to us during the writing of this book.

Finally, we would like to thank the first director of the Iowa Regents' Center for Early Developmental Education, Dr. Judith Finkelstein, for continuing her support of the work that is being done at the center, and the late Dr. Rheta DeVries for leading us in our journey to become constructivist educators. We would like to acknowledge our editor, Dr. Beth Dykstra Van Meeteren, for her continued confidence in us and our work. These three women have inspired us through their leadership, insights, support, and friendship.

FOUNDATIONS OF INQUIRY LEARNING AND TEACHING WITH INFANTS AND TODDLERS

Many adults who spend time with very young children will have observed their actions as humorous, at best, or superficial with little intentional thinking, at worst. Children's preference for repeating actions may become so frustrating for some adults that they end their engagement with the child. However, adults who observe closely and develop an understanding of what the infants or toddlers are doing can also develop an understanding of learning through inquiry. In addition, those observations will support educators in finding ways to enhance opportunities for each and every child, regardless of their developmental stage, cultural background, or approach to learning.

Part I of this book is designed to support adults, whether they are educators, family members, or others, in gaining understanding of how very young children may respond to people or materials. We do this in three ways:

- Explaining how young children think about their world and attempt to solve the problems they discover there. Years of observations, conversations, and reading have led us to a broad understanding of very young children's learning through inquiry. While infants and toddlers have been doing inquiry forever, we are just now beginning to understand how they do so. We explain that process through the Infant Toddler Inquiry Learning Model in Chapter 1.

- Supporting learning through inquiry, with the knowledge that all aspects of children's development are affected by their environments, including physical, social–emotional, intellectual, and invitational environments. Across all environments, we note that positive relationships between educators and infants or toddlers is the first priority.

- Elevating the work of adults who work with infants and toddlers as a respected component of the education system through deliberate planning, observation, and assessment of the learning that occurs throughout the day. We see that process as the foundation of respect and support for very young children and their educators. We also advocate for opportunities for educators to engage with peers, administrators, and outside professional development experiences that can enhance their work.

CHAPTER 1

Introduction

Inquiry Learning and Teaching With Infants and Toddlers

Jill Uhlenberg

WHO WE ARE

We are former and current infant or toddler educators who remain dedicated to supporting others in the field through expanding ideas about infants and toddlers, their needs, their development, their interests, and their thinking about the world. We are continually trying out new materials with very young children to develop high-quality curriculum because we believe that early STEM matters (Spaepen et al., 2017). We have taught other adults, in higher education, professional development trainings, conference presentations, and classroom coaching or mentoring, as well as in writing, about what we have learned from the young ones. Because we have been where you are in the classroom or home setting, we designed this book to offer new insights about your work. Some of the ideas you read here will be familiar, and some may be new for you. We view learning as a process. We support your learning, but we also expect to learn through the process of writing of this book.

WHO WE HOPE YOU ARE

If you are working with infants or toddlers in any capacity, we hope you will find this book helpful. You might be a parent or grandparent, a child development home provider, an educator working with a group of infants or toddlers in child care or Early Head Start, a home interventionist, or someone who works with children 0–3 in another capacity or setting. We consider you an educator of infants or toddlers and use that term throughout this book. As an infant or toddler educator, your background and education may be anywhere within a wide span of training or preparation, from high school through college, or mainly from experience. Our goal in this book is to support you and to honor your work as an educator of this most important group of children.

WHO WE ARE WRITING ABOUT

We are passionate about the youngest children, those from birth through toddlerhood. Over time, we have become passionate about STEM as well, and have noticed the lack of STEM experiences intentionally offered for this age group. In reality, most infant or toddler educators do offer STEM experiences, many without realizing it. We hope to elevate that in this book.

We discuss this age group throughout the chapters and generally divide the groups into three categories as we describe their experiences with a variety of materials. Your definitions and terms may be different from ours, but we are all talking about the same children, including those with special needs, or language or cultural differences. Rather than dividing only by age, we have chosen to share our experiences with children in these three categories:

- Young infants, who are generally not yet mobile. These children are more reliant on the adults to provide the materials and to support their physical ability to explore. They are usually under 12 months old.

- Young toddlers, who are walking or at least moving around without adult support. Typically, this group is in the process of learning language and is approximately 12–24 months old.
- Older toddlers, who are typically quite self-sufficient, carry on conversations, ask questions, and move easily and exuberantly around their space. These children are approximately 24–36 months old.

We find that very young children will act upon objects depending on their prior experiences rather than their ages. An older toddler may use the same exploratory strategies as a mobile infant when new materials are offered. We also noticed that within the birth–3 group, individual differences in development may vary quite substantially, depending on any special needs or language development, and among children whose home language is not English. The culture of the educational setting also is variable, with educators responding in different ways to different children. We encourage educators to give power to the children to explore and experience materials rather than trying to meet assumed expectations for a specific task at a specific age.

Alyssa's vignette describes an experience with a very young girl who clearly has thoughts about what she has experienced in her play. The adult is surprised at the communication possible with an infant.

> ### Textbox 1.1. Alyssa Watches the Trees
>
> At 8 months old, Alyssa was not yet walking. She sat on the floor in front of a musical toy, pushed a button on the toy, and listened to a short musical melody. She repeated her action many times and smiled. Each time the music started, she spread her arms and swiveled her upper body first in one direction, then the other, until the music stopped. She repeated this action several times, smiling each time at Jill, the adult seated on the floor next to her. Jill began to imitate Alyssa's movements, arms out, swiveling with the music. She said, "We are dancing!" and then repeated, "Dance, dance" each time Alyssa started the music.
>
> Later, Alyssa sat on Jill's lap. They both looked out a large window, watching dark clouds move and the strong wind blow trees. The trees waved back and forth as the wind blew. Alyssa looked at Jill, then at the trees, then at Jill again. She pointed at the trees, and then moved her body in the same swivel she had used when listening to the music. Jill smiled and remarked, "Yes, the trees are dancing!" (see Figure 1.1).

Our experiences with infants and toddlers have convinced us that these very young children are thinking all the time. Observations of them and their actions are vital to understanding their thinking. We are often surprised by their understanding and creativity. We hope that this book will support your care and understanding as well.

Figure 1.1. Alyssa Watches the Trees

WHAT IS INQUIRY?

An Internet search of the term *inquiry* yields a remarkable 135 million hits. The online Merriam-Webster (n.d.) dictionary definition reads:

A request for information;
A systematic investigation often of a matter of public interest;
An examination of facts or principles: Research.

Even as adults, we continue the process of learning new ideas or connections every day. We do this through the development of preconceptions, or early ideas of understanding a concept or a relationship. Through experience, we modify those preconceptions to a new level, sometimes repeating the modification process over time, and sometimes reaching a full and accurate understanding of that concept. This does not always occur, however, even as we become adults.

An educator once complained about the cold weather we were experiencing and explained that the "windshield factor" was well below 0 degrees that day. When asked to explain this statement, she described her concept of the coldness of the wind as based on some measurement taken by weather professionals using some device attached to their vehicle's windshield. This preconception of the "wind chill factor" was an attempt at understanding the world, but it was clearly an understanding still in the process of becoming accurate.

Jean Piaget studied young children to understand how they learned about the world around them. His work was a foundation for much of what we know today about education. Piaget (1954) called the process of learning *constructing knowledge* because he believed that humans control that process internally. He described three kinds of knowledge that exist:

- Physical knowledge
- Logical-mathematical knowledge
- Cultural or social knowledge

The first kind of knowledge Piaget termed physical knowledge, which is the set of properties of objects that we experience through our senses—texture, size, shape, and so on. The second kind of knowledge Piaget described is logical-mathematical knowledge, which is based on the relationships that exist between two or more objects (or people). Dr. Rheta DeVries, a student of Piaget, used to describe these two kinds of knowledge as two sides of the same coin because they are closely related. Once we have physical knowledge about something, we can begin to explore the relationships of those characteristics by flipping back and forth between our physical knowledge and logical-mathematical knowledge constructions.

As an example, we can examine what we know about a tennis ball—what it is and does. We use our senses to determine the physical knowledge of the ball—fuzzy, round, with seams or lines that join the parts, and bouncy. It may have a smell or taste to it. Then our logical-mathematical knowledge allows us to see how it bounces when we throw it different ways. If I throw it forcefully on the floor, it bounces higher than when I drop it—a relationship between my action and the ball's bounciness. If I roll it on the floor, it does not bounce at all until it hits something solid. Piaget tells us that these preconceptions or constructions about tennis balls are the result of experience. The more experiences we have with the materials, the more we understand the relationships and the more accurate our conceptions are. We make sense of the world of tennis balls.

Of course, other people can tell us the information, but young children tend to hear this information skeptically. They want and need experience to construct that knowledge—that is, to believe it. Even adults will not always believe information provided by someone else. For example, a *wet paint* sign may not prevent us from touching a newly painted object. For very young children, the whole world is subject to engagement and exploration so they can construct these two kinds of knowledge. The more physical knowledge we construct, the more relationships we can uncover or develop and understand. This is inquiry.

Many people work through an inquiry approach. Doctors have a base of knowledge. When they discover a problem or symptom with a patient, they gather information and make a diagnosis. If that symptom is unusual or outside their knowledge base, they perform tests and gather data to solve the problem. That's inquiry. Educators work through inquiry, many without realizing it. We observe children and identify problems with their learning; try strategies, gathering data as we go; and work to solve the learning problem. Again, that's inquiry.

The third kind of knowledge is cultural or social knowledge, such as the name we give an object. This knowledge is passed from one person to another. Returning to the tennis ball, it may be yellow, which we can see, but we need a name for that color, which varies in different cultures or languages. Calling the ball a "tennis ball" is cultural knowledge, with different words used in other languages. How to play tennis with its rules is also cultural or social knowledge because we cannot know the rules without someone telling us. This kind of knowledge is passed from person to person rather than being constructed internally. We teach infants and toddlers the names of things, providing the cultural knowledge, so that we can communicate with one another about those objects.

The question is, What does inquiry look like among infants and toddlers?

WHAT WE MEAN BY INQUIRY LEARNING AND TEACHING

Warden (2021) notes four approaches to inquiry teaching and learning. She describes them as:

- Free inquiry—children are empowered to select the inquiry and the adult supports the process
- Guided inquiry—adults select the inquiry and children explore in their own ways
- Controlled inquiry—adults choose the inquiry and provide the resources to solve the problems
- Structured inquiry—children follow the lead of the adult as they all do the same inquiry (p. 4)

Our approach is the first type. That is, we strongly believe that children should be the first line in deciding what to explore. For infants and toddlers, this may expand into guided inquiry as adults select materials. However, whenever possible, materials should be chosen based on children's interests that educators have observed.

Educators should be aware that guided inquiry, with adults selecting the topic to be explored, may result in children choosing not to engage with the materials presented to them. Educators who know their children well will notice when materials spark curiosity, and they will pursue those interests with the children. Educators also will notice when children lose interest quickly and seek other activities. This is a sign that adults have not selected materials that engage the children, or that the children may be pressured to follow the adult's lead.

When adults select both the materials and the problems to be solved, as in controlled or structured inquiry, older children often will comply to please the adults. Infants and toddlers, however, have not yet seen the need to fake interest. Infants may signal disinterest through fussing or falling asleep, and toddlers simply may move on to other materials. In this book you will read about many experiences we have had with these very young children as they explored materials for long periods of time over many days.

Some educators suggest that inquiry is a cycle, or that learning can be described as a trajectory where all children engage in activities in the same set of steps or even in the same sequence. Free inquiry describes a set of actions or strategies that engage children in learning based on their interests. This means that although actions or materials used may look similar among different children, it is more likely that actions and explorations will vary from one child to the next because they are interested in different things. For inquiry to be successful, adults must accept this seemingly messy approach while children are learning. This process is explained in the next section, where we share our view of how infants and toddlers learn.

INFANT TODDLER INQUIRY LEARNING MODEL

Few researchers (Hoisington et al., 2014; Stacey, 2019) have described a model for how young children engage in inquiry learning in preschool or primary grades. Even fewer have described what inquiry learning looks like for children birth to 3 years old. This age group may be preverbal or still gaining the ability to communicate their thoughts, so the inquiry process may not include any verbalized communication. We may have to guess or deduce what the child is thinking or what their goal is at any time, based on their actions. In addition, the youngest children, who are not yet mobile, must rely on the adults to provide the materials before they can begin to explore.

We think about what infants and toddlers do when confronted with new materials that invite their interest. In our observations, we see children who have sustained interest and try multiple strategies to attain their goals. This observation conflicts with the general perception that very young children have short attention spans. We find that given ample time and interesting materials, as well as trusting the children to learn through their choice of materials and actions, infants and toddlers demonstrate an amazing attention span. Sometimes the child's interest is not what we have planned or expected, such as when a toddler spends more time examining a box than its contents. Some adults consider this to be simply cute and playful; however, some of us recognize that the toddler is exploring ideas of spatial understanding or the strength of a cardboard construction.

Wonder. When educators present new materials, the youngest children typically begin inquiry by exploring physical characteristics in the wonder process. Young infants will gaze at the materials, then move their bodies excitedly as educators move the items around. The infants may reach and grasp materials. Older infants may mouth, shake, strike, or throw items as they wonder. The more familiar the children become with the materials, the more they begin to try out different strategies to see what happens. Children who have had enough experiences with the materials to gain physical knowledge—based on the children's concept of enough—then will invent and try new strategies and observe what happens. Or the children may just consider their initial perceptions and repeat the same actions again.

We observed toddlers who worked with specific materials one day, then returned to the same materials and actions on succeeding days. They appeared to remember what they were doing and thinking, and we wondered whether their time away was used as an incubation period, allowing them to consider, or reconsider, their perceptions. Toddlers may spend less time in the wonder process and move more rapidly to the exploration of materials. Or they may start their experience in the strategize process, as their mobility allows them more freedom in inventing new actions.

Strategize. As the children strategize, they discover or create problems that are interesting to them. Ample time and supportive adults encourage children to solve the problems they find, without the adults providing solutions. Strategizing, using materials in different ways, may lead to solutions, or the children may decide to leave these materials and engage with something else.

Resolve. Children also may show persistence, eventually resolving their chosen problems. The solution may or may not be one that the adults would consider to be correct. If the child appears to be satisfied, we need to accept that approximation, because the solution is a notable step on the way to the adult's perception of correct. Children may repeat their resolution process as confirmation that they accomplished what they set out to do. Returning to the same materials later also affirms the child's problem-solving abilities.

Older toddlers may wish to demonstrate their solution to another child or to an adult, but many will opt to just continue their inquiry with new materials. Observation of children's efforts is important in the inquiry process so that educators can understand children's actions and thinking. These observations also may show that the child is engaged in more than one part of the process at a time. That is, the child's actions may appear to be wondering, strategizing, and resolution at the same time. The blurred lines seem to be part of the way these youngest children think about the world as integrated rather than being divided into different domains.

Processes Overlap. The inquiry process is not linear, as demonstrated in the model by the overlapping circles (see Figure 1.2). That is, the infants and toddlers move freely within the processes as they engage with materials, gaining physical knowledge, exploring, constructing logical-mathematical knowledge, and reflecting about what they have experienced; deciding whether to repeat their actions; trying new strategies; stopping to think for a while; or leaving or ignoring the materials altogether. If the child has not accepted the solution to

Figure 1.2. Infant Toddler Inquiry Learning Model

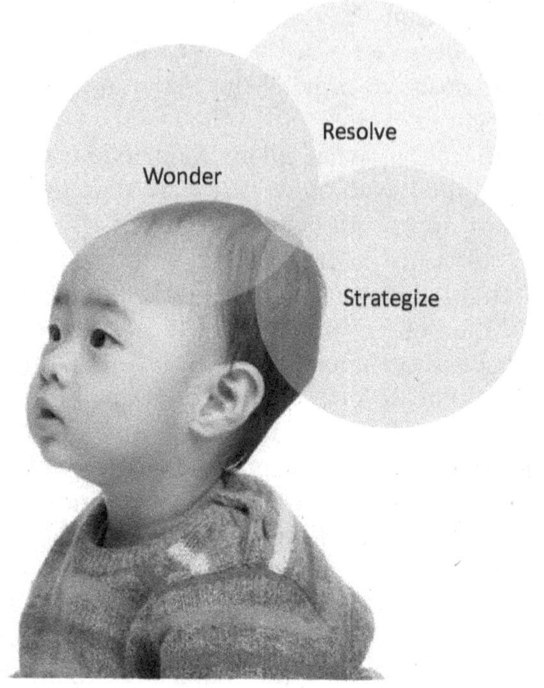

® Iowa Regents' Center for Early Developmental Education. Photo 39158520 © Leung Cho Pan | Dreamstime.com.

a problem, revisiting that problem with new strategies or materials extends the inquiry process until the child reaches an acceptable resolution, even if that resolution is to leave the problem behind.

Older toddlers may communicate their thinking more openly than infants or young toddlers, because older children's communication skills are generally better developed. Young children with language delays or who experience languages other than English at home also may speak less about what they are doing. This means the educators must be more observant in trying to understand what the children are thinking or why they are trying certain strategies on the materials. We can guess about their thinking, but sometimes we don't know. Continued observations with good note-taking can help educators in understanding this part of the inquiry process. Talking to other educators also can support our understanding.

You will become better at this understanding as you have more experience with the children and the materials. By the way, when you do this, you are using the inquiry process yourself to study the children's work through inquiry.

We know how much young children enjoy repetition of many events and actions—reading the same books over and over, banging a toy on a hard or soft surface, dropping food or utensils to the floor from their chair, and so on. This is why we recommend allowing extended time over many days for children to fully engage, explore, think about, and reengage with materials. Sometimes the wondering is about whether the same things will happen today that happened before. If the materials are the same and my actions are the same, will the result be the same? As adults, we accept these outcomes as regular, but very young children may lack the history to support those conclusions. How much history is enough to make an event regular? Only the children know.

> **TEXTBOX 1.2. KALEA PLACES A BALL IN A MUFFIN TIN**
>
> Amelia, a toddler educator, sat next to 14-month-old Kalea. Kalea was attempting to place a fabric ball in a muffin tin cup that Amelia was holding. After Kalea

inserted the ball successfully into one cup at the end of the muffin tin, she moved the same ball carefully into each of the 12 separate cups in the muffin tin, pushing the ball into each cup to see whether it would fit. Amelia remarked, "You are putting the ball in the muffin tin. Does the ball fit in there? And there? And there?" Amelia repeated this same question patiently as Kalea moved the ball into successive muffin cups one by one.

While Amelia observed Kalea's exploration of the ball and muffin tin, she noted Kalea's hesitation before moving the ball each time. Her questions supported Kalea's actions and allowed Kalea the time to fully consider the relationship between the ball and the muffin tin.

The Infant Toddler Inquiry Learning Model is a way to think about how very young children participate in exploratory experiences as they engage with the world. If we observe and think about their actions, we can understand more clearly how to support their learning. The Inquiry Teaching Model, described below, explains how educators can support infants and toddlers, or even older children, in the inquiry process by focusing on the educator's role in inquiry learning.

INQUIRY TEACHING MODEL

When we are thinking about what inquiry looks like for very young children, we also ask what inquiry looks like among infant and toddler educators. Many of those 135 million Internet hits about inquiry are focused on the system for educators to manage inquiry in their classrooms or educational settings. In other words, the models describe how to teach through an inquiry approach. Most of these models are geared toward learners substantially older than 8 years old. Instead, we use the ITM developed at the Regents' Center for Early Developmental Education at the University of Northern Iowa and published in the book *STEM Learning With Young Children* (Counsell et al., 2016), which is based on our experiences with early childhood educators of children from pre-K–3rd grade. We have found that this teaching model applies just as well to educators of children, birth–3.

Both the ITILM and ITM models are nonlinear. That is, the arrows in the Inquiry Teaching Model

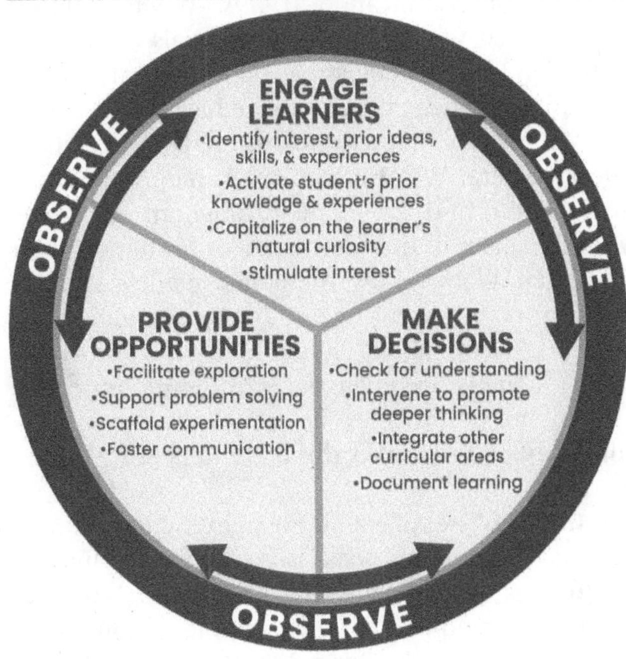

Figure 1.3. Inquiry Teaching Model

Note. Adapted from Counsell et al. (2016).

indicate that the process varies depending on the child, the educator, and the materials they are exploring (see Figure 1.3).

The ITM is similar to the ITILM above. However, where the ITILM describes what the infants and toddlers do, the ITM describes what the educators do. While older children and adults learning through inquiry can manage their actions and seek out materials on their own, infants and toddlers must rely more substantially on the adults around them. The most basic role of the educator is to provide interesting materials. Dr. Rheta DeVries was noted for her approach: "What is there in this activity for children to figure out? If there isn't much to figure out, then it may not be worthy of children's time" (DeVries, personal communication, 2001). Even infants and toddlers deserve interesting and thought-provoking materials. Without those materials, that perceived short attention span takes over, frustrating both children and educators.

Dr. Judith Finkelstein, founder of the Iowa Regents' Center for Early Developmental Education, also remarked about the need for high-quality experiences for young children. Her mantra addressed the relationship between curriculum and guidance or discipline in the early childhood classroom: "The best guidance is a good curriculum" (Finkelstein, personal communication, 1989). When children are engaged with interesting materials offered for extended time periods, the need for educator intervention to manage behavior is reduced.

We provide a description of the components of the ITM here. We also include examples of educators' actions and comments throughout the STEM focus chapters in this book in order to support your understanding of how these two models support each other. We even suggest that adults who spend time "messing about" with materials (Hawkins, 1965) actually are engaging in the same processes that infants and toddlers do as they explore materials. Chapter 3 describes this more in depth.

Observe. The role of observation is vitally important in inquiry, and especially when the children are under 3 years old. Many are preverbal, not yet speaking, or nonverbal, or unwilling to communicate through speech. This may be due to a child's lack of vocabulary to describe their actions or thinking, a language delay, a case of dual-language learning, or just because the child does not wish to speak about their experiences. In addition, some very young children will choose to speak with one adult, but not others. Observations lead and support the other parts of the process. In addition, observations are vital in all forms of assessment, as well as in reporting learning to parents, administrators, or others. You will read more about observation in Chapter 3.

Engage Learners. While infants and toddlers engage willingly with any new materials, educators can provide materials that invite exploration and encourage learning. Young infants are limited in their ability to explore unless educators place materials within view or reach. Toddlers will explore any new materials they see within the environment. Observation will support educators in understanding the limits of engagement or fatigue of the children, so educators can provide new materials or ask questions that stimulate additional explorations.

Even though infants and toddlers may not verbalize their questions, they still have questions as they try to understand how the world works (Greenfield et al., 2017). Observations can direct us to understanding what those specific questions are.

Provide Opportunities. Providing materials and observing the children's actions allows educators opportunities to build vocabulary. The same observations will provide information about children's struggles to reach their goals, allowing the educator to expand on ideas and scaffold or support explorations. Using self-talk or parallel talk supports preverbal children in their beginning attempts at language. In self-talk, educators describe their own actions as they perform them. You may have heard an educator narrate their steps as they change a diaper or prepare some materials. In parallel talk, the educator describes the child's actions as they happen. Beyond simple communication, these strategies support children's thinking and understanding. Educators also enhance opportunities to learn when they provide comments or ask open-ended questions to support children's explorations.

Make Decisions. Children's engagement or lack of it, noted through observation, supports the educator in deciding whether to add or delete materials, suggest observing another child's approach, or simply watch without interfering. When a child becomes frustrated, the educator must decide how much to intercede. We hold specific beliefs about allowing the children to problem-solve on their own without telling them what to do. There are strategies, however, that can support children in their problem solving without just telling them the answers to their questions.

Teaching through inquiry means teaching with intention. As you read through the ITM, you can see within each section where educators are working intentionally to support children's learning through engaging with curriculum and materials and through decision-making about how to proceed. Educators' actions support the children's construction of both physical knowledge and logical-mathematical knowledge, and, when appropriate, educators provide cultural knowledge through their interactions with the children. There are multiple opportunities for enhancing communication skills as educators provide labels for new items, offer encouragement for explorations, and ask questions that guide the children's focus on what happens.

In each chapter in this book, we describe a child's or children's actions with materials and discuss how the ITILM engages the child or children in the process of inquiry. Then we include a discussion of the ITM, where you read about the educator's actions, comments, or other engagements with the children as they explore materials.

Figure 1.4. Jonah Investigates Flashlights

TEXTBOX 1.3. JONAH CATCHES A LIGHT

The Cubs (12 months to 24 months) investigated a variety of human-made light sources. Valerie selected a small LED light and pushed the switch repeatedly in order to produce a light. Niles found a large flashlight and attempted to activate it by moving the toggle switch to the "on" position. Coen picked up several flashlights, carefully looked them over, then selected one. Jonah tried several flashlights before finding one that he could activate easily. He moved the beam around after turning the light on and stopped when the educator called his attention to the "spot" he made on the wall. He brought his flashlight to another adult to demonstrate the on–off switch. He directed the light to the ceiling so that he and the adults could see a circle of light. Jonah grinned at the educator when she pointed to the ceiling and commented, "You made a circle with your flashlight."

Jonah looked down to see the circle of light on the floor and walked toward it. He took a large step as if to stomp on the circle of light. He looked up and said, "I did it!" He moved toward the toy shelves, shined the light on the floor, and tried again to place his foot on the circle of light. He looked up and again said, "I did it!" The educator noticed his interest in stepping on the spots and commented, "Jonah, you stepped on that spot!" Jonah looked up, grinned at the adult, then continued his investigation.

He shined the light on the toys on the shelf and then moved closer to the other children and adults. As he walked near her, an educator handed him a box, and he shined the light inside.

He continued to walk around the room with the flashlight and tried it on a variety of toys that were in his path. Two of the adults noticed Jonah when he was close to them. They made eye contact and smiled but let him continue the investigation without commenting or interrupting his investigation.

Jonah and the Infant Toddler Inquiry Learning Model

Jonah investigated the Light and Shadow materials that were made available to him in his toddler classroom. He used familiar strategies first in his attempts to turn on flashlights, then he tried some different strategies before experiencing success. He noticed that the spot on the floor made by the flashlight was just in front of his foot. He tried to place his foot on the spot by taking a wide stride but had difficulty hitting the spot the first time he attempted to step on it. He observed the results of his investigation and then tried a new strategy by changing the position of the spot and the length of his stride to get them to match up. When his new strategy worked so that he was able to step on the spot, he looked at the adult nearest him and said, "I did it!" to communicate to her that he had successfully accomplished his goal. He continued his investigation by using the flashlight to illuminate other materials in his classroom so he could observe the effect on them. He continued to change the targets of his light and observe the results.

Jonah's Educator and the Inquiry Teaching Model

This toddler educator provided her toddler class with engaging materials that could be investigated over time. She provided support with her close proximity to the children as they explored the flashlights in her darkened classroom. She acknowledged Jonah's accomplishments by noticing them and commenting but did not distract him with questions. She scanned the room frequently during her observation of Jonah's investigation to determine whether other children needed her support. When she observed that all of the children were engaged with the Light and Shadow materials, she began to document what the children were doing by snapping photos, video recording, and jotting notes about the exploration that the children were engaged in around the classroom. During her planned work time, she will upload the photos and video so she can use her documentation for her assessment system, to communicate progress with parents, and to plan for future learning opportunities with Light and Shadow materials. Her careful observations of Jonah's learning informed her that he would benefit from more time with the flashlights, but that he soon will be ready for additional challenges. After sharing observations with her colleagues, she decided to keep the flashlights in baskets on the toy shelves for at least 2 weeks and to add the overhead projector to center time at the beginning of the following week. Educator-made laminated overlays with a variety of colored paper and ribbon, plastic chains, plastic binder dividers, and handheld color palettes also would be added to the center for children to investigate. She included standards in her lesson plans so that parents and visitors would know what to watch for while in the classroom. She shared photos and documentation with families in her newsletter so they would be able to support high-quality learning at home.

WHAT WE MEAN BY STEM

STEM is an acronym for science, technology, engineering, and mathematics. The Boston Children's Museum has developed definitions for the four areas in thinking about how they look when infants and toddlers engage in STEM.

- Science is exploring materials and making predictions based on observations.
- Technology is using tools, being inventive, identifying problems, and building materials.
- Engineering is solving problems, using a variety of materials, designing and creating, and building things that work.
- Mathematics is a way of measuring, sequencing, patterning, and exploring shapes, spaces, volume, and size. (Adapted from Boston Children's Museum, 2013, p. 3)

We have explored several STEM focus areas with very young children and share those experiences in this book. We find that all four STEM areas are included in most of the experiences we describe. Infants and toddlers do not separate them. We find that their efforts are more engaging as integrated curriculum than if we tried to describe them separately, although we may bring a particular focus to your attention.

WHY WE WROTE THIS BOOK

Our goal in writing this book was to provide support for educators in their work with infants and toddlers. In our work, we note that many educators struggle with ideas for providing interesting and engaging curriculum materials for this age group. Many books have been written that suggest what we call a one-and-done approach to STEM, such as in the controlled inquiry or structured inquiry approaches (Warden, 2021), and that is likely related to that short attention span we mentioned above. Some educators, and many curriculum developers, assume that infants or toddlers will not stay engaged for long, so the activities merely become times to put out materials for a brief period and then clean up. The approach we write about in this book involves time and plenty of it. Our experiences have shown clearly that toddlers will stay busy with interesting materials for an hour or more every day, over several weeks. If interest begins to wane, simple additions or switching out items can regenerate interest. We include multiple examples of young children we have seen engaged with materials. Using an inquiry approach provides much-needed time and encouragement to the children in exploring STEM topics. Some commercial or informally posted digital STEM curricula provide brief activities that do not allow for the depth of learning that an inquiry approach provides.

When possible, we try to use materials that are inexpensive and easy to obtain. Safety of materials is always the first consideration, but we also know that infant and toddler programs often are the least supported financially because some people think this age group is not important to a child's lifelong learning experience. We know otherwise. When possible, we suggest ways to provide interesting materials without the need for additional funds.

We try to infuse concepts of inclusion throughout the book, knowing that children with special needs often are not yet identified at this young age. However, the variety of materials we describe is intended to serve Universal Design for Learning (UDL) elements (Center for Applied Special Technology [CAST], 2018), which consider the unevenness of children's abilities in any environment. This is done by considering: (1) the why of learning, (2) the what of learning, and (3) the how of learning. Because these learning characteristics are just forming within infants and toddlers, we suggest many ways to engage and support these very young children through selection of materials and teaching strategies that enhance the efforts of all children.

STEM covers a wide spectrum of topics. We have not explored them all with these very young children, but we have selected those that seem to be most interesting to the children we engage with. We have explored some topics more fully than others. If your children find a topic you want to try, we encourage you to do so. Hopefully, this book will support you in that process.

The explorations in this book clearly and effectively address standards in STEM areas, as well as in other areas of development. We have been regularly surprised at the amount of understanding children have constructed, especially the depth and breadth of that learning. Our goals in writing this book and the other STEM books in our series are to support educators in their inquiry of teaching in general, and STEM topics in particular. We hope to encourage educators to observe the learning that is already taking place and to document that learning as a record for parents, colleagues, and administrators. In the process, educators can experience the joy of working with infants and toddlers.

Infants and toddlers think like scientists. They explore, hypothesize, try things out, and rethink when their results are not satisfactory. We encourage you to think like scientists in your work. Explore the materials yourself, observe how children use them, hypothesize on what they are thinking and learning, try ideas that support or challenge children's thinking, and then analyze your observations as you rethink what you thought you knew about infants and toddlers.

CHAPTER 2

Preparing the Environment for Inquiry With Infants and Toddlers

Sherri Peterson and Jill Uhlenberg

An environment that promotes inquiry for infants and toddlers is intentional. The educators are responsive to each child's unique needs, the physical environment is designed so that children can investigate and explore without unnecessary intervention, the visual spaces provide a sense of belonging and invite discovery, and planned experiences are based on observations of children's interests and an understanding of their growing competence.

TEXTBOX 2.1. KYLIE AND ANDREA PLAY WOODEN BLOCKS

Andrea, an educator, and Kylie (21 months) were sitting near the sound materials that had been set out for children to investigate. The materials included tin cans and wooden blocks. Kylie selected a small block and began to tap the back of the toy shelves with her block. Andrea began to imitate Kylie's actions. When Kylie saw that Andrea was following her lead, she changed her actions by speeding up the tapping. Andrea quickly responded by tapping faster. Kylie's eyes lit up when she realized that she had the power to influence the play. She tapped more loudly, and Andrea labeled the sounds they were making "loud." Kylie responded by tapping more quietly, looked at Andrea, and whispered "soft." Kylie leaned down and smiled broadly at Andrea, who said, "Was that fun?" Kylie slipped around the shelf unit and continued with her tapping and labeling her actions—fast and slow, loud and soft. Andrea continued to allow Kylie to lead the interaction until Kylie tired of the game.

This "serve and return" continued for several rounds (see Figure 2.1).

In this exchange, Andrea demonstrated a powerful interaction that built on the trusting relationship she had fostered with Kylie. When adults share an authentic connection with children, there is a foundation for inquiry. As Kylie investigated the new materials, Andrea observed from a distance to allow Kylie to select something that was of interest to her and to wonder about the possibilities of the wooden block she had chosen. She understood that Kylie often finds a quiet place away from other children for exploration when new materials are available.

Figure 2.1. Making Sounds With Blocks

When Kylie launched her sound investigation, Andrea moved quietly to her side, and then connected with her by making eye contact and picking up another block. Based on her understanding of Kylie's unique personality and ways of learning, Andrea interacted with Kylie by following her lead as she tried out both old and new strategies with her block. When Andrea observed that Kylie was eager to continue the interaction, she extended the learning by labeling the sounds—loud, soft, fast, slow. Kylie responded by labeling her own soft tapping. Kylie watched Andrea for her reactions when she moved to the other side of the shelves and continued to tap the shelf. Kylie communicated her satisfaction with the exploration and the actions she and Andrea had taken, by continuing the "dance" and then creating a new problem to be addressed. Andrea continued the interaction until Kylie indicated that she had resolved her inquiry.

THE INFANT AND TODDLER ENVIRONMENT: CREATING AN ENVIRONMENT THAT INVITES INQUIRY

Our understanding about the impact of the environment on children's healthy development has come from many sources within the early childhood community—both past and present. We have worked in licensed infant and toddler programs that use quality rating scales and program standards to guide educators on interactions among people, health and safety procedures, curriculum, materials and equipment, and use of space. While these guidelines are important and sometimes necessary for programs to be licensed or accredited, we also recognize that an environment that invites inquiry requires more than a checklist of how many blocks are on the shelves or how meals are prepared and served. "The physical environment exerts its influence not only on the educational activities through intentional planning but also through non-intentional and incidental elements" (Knauf, 2019, p. 358).

As we thought about what inquiry for infants and toddlers means for us, we thought about how the environment can support children in this age group with a classroom design that is responsive to children's developmental needs and a place where they can be active participants in their learning as they make their own discoveries. And because we have spent time in many classrooms over the past several decades, we thought about ways that environments can be transformed in order to provide more opportunities for inquiry.

The notion that the environment can be a powerful influence on children's learning has long been recognized by early childhood leaders, researchers, and practitioners. That the setting actually can be part of the curriculum has been illuminated in the schools of Reggio Emilia, Italy. In Reggio Emilia programs, the environment is described as the third educator (Gandini, 1998), and Reggio and Reggio-inspired classrooms are aesthetically pleasing, showcase children's work, and offer provocations for inquiry. The environment should suggest a sense of belonging, a sense of well-being, and an invitation for engagement. The environment is the context in which all connections are made; this includes connections among the people who inhabit the space and the mental connections that are the basis for learning.

Nurturing a classroom community that invites inquiry is an ongoing process and requires a commitment from program administrators so that educators of infants and toddlers have opportunities for planning and collaboration. In effective programs for young children, educators have time away from their classroom responsibilities to share insights and observations about individual children and their needs, voice their personal perspectives about the classroom culture and curriculum, develop activities and experiences, and participate in professional learning. When educators have dedicated time to work collaboratively and grow professionally, they feel valued. This contributes to the healthy climate of the program and of individual classrooms. Administrators in thriving programs recognize the value of collaboration and consult with educators about materials and classroom expenditures, family engagement, professional development needs, and long-range plans. Educators who are on the front lines can provide valuable insight about the children and families being served. When given opportunities to contribute their point of view, they can be the program's greatest asset.

Environments are powerful. They can welcome children and families by honoring their cultures and communities. They can provide security when children are uncertain. They can inspire exploration by providing spaces that are inviting and materials that are open-ended. And they can be extraordinary places where children thrive and adults are supported in their important work.

THE SOCIAL–EMOTIONAL ATMOSPHERE: CREATING AN ENVIRONMENT OF YES

A significant body of research teaches us that supportive interactions actually can shape the brain by increasing the number of neural connections that lead to social, emotional, language, and intellectual competence. The connections that are formed provide either a strong or a weak foundation for the connections that form later. "As young children develop, their early emotional experiences literally become embedded in the architecture of their brains" (National Scientific Council on the Developing Child, 2004, p. 1). Serve-and-return interactions between children and the adults who care for them are essential for forming the architecture of the brain. In this example we see Andrea engage in a serve-and-return interaction with Kylie when she tunes in to Kylie's gestures and expressions, and counters with a timely and sensitive response. Early brain development is directly influenced by interactions with significant adults who understand that infants and toddlers are both vulnerable and competent, and that these two attributes must be addressed in concert with each other (Lally & Mangione, 2017). *Relationships are at the heart of an inquiry learning environment.* When adults recognize the connection between relationships and learning, the foundation for inquiry is strengthened and the opportunity for each child to meet their potential is possible.

Social–emotional development is closely tied to the environments in which young children live, and it can be influenced by the interactions they observe among the significant people around them. These building blocks for a nurturing environment begin with the adult relationships in the classroom. To feel secure, infants and toddlers need a safe and predictable base for exploration. Tension or conflict in the adult relationships can be an obstacle for learning. Adults have a responsibility for creating and maintaining an emotionally healthy and harmonious classroom. Educators who nurture the adult relationships within the classroom, and come to a shared understanding about how they want the classroom to be, are better prepared to support their interactions with children.

Respectful adult interactions provide a foundation of security that can promote inquiry. Inquiry is further supported when individual differences and rates of learning are recognized, planned experiences acknowledge differences in dispositions, and the classroom environment represents all of the adults and children. The educator's view of the child as a competent, capable, and curious learner is front and center in an environment that is ready for inquiry.

An environment that is ready for inquiry is a place where

- children recognize themselves, their families, and their communities in the artifacts that are selected for display;
- children can explore and investigate without interference in a place that is safe and secure;
- the classroom arrangement and the materials selected for children have been tested by adults to determine whether they provide the possibility for inquiry;
- children have choices;
- centers visible to children are always available;
- items intended for adult use are out of reach or behind closed doors;
- routines are predictable and schedules are flexible to allow educators to capitalize on children's interests;
- children are viewed as competent and have opportunities to connect new ideas to what they already know and can do;
- educators support rather than intervene, and pay close attention to what children are doing in order to understand;
- there is mutual trust—the child trusts the educator to give full attention and the educator trusts the child to solve some of their own problems; and
- adults explain what children can do, not what they can't do.

Responsive environments include consideration of children's unique developmental needs, interests, and emerging skills. The evidence is irrefutable that for infants and toddlers, all learning happens in the context of nurturing and responsive interactions with adults who are important to them. Feeling a sense of belonging to a group sets children up for success as learners.

Environments that promote inquiry offer young children the opportunity to make choices and direct their own learning, provide effective encouragement for emotion regulation, and include scaffolding that provides support and practice for emerging skills before the children are expected to manage them independently (Center on the Developing Child, 2011). Finding a balance between the promotion of cognitive and academic learning and social–emotional competencies is the responsibility of early childhood programs. In order for children to wonder about the materials provided for them, strategize possible solutions to problems they have discovered, and resolve these problems or create new problems to be solved, they must be securely attached to adults who understand the importance of observing and connecting with them. A classroom ready for inquiry is thoughtful and intentional, and has regard for children's innate curiosity, wonder, and joy in all the decisions that are made.

THE INVITATIONAL ENVIRONMENT: CREATING A PLACE THAT SAYS "I BELONG"

In our years of learning with young children, we have had the privilege of visiting classrooms where the attention to children's learning and their sense of belonging is clearly visible. In classrooms where the focus is clear, this invitational environment communicates that what children know and can do is celebrated and valued. Our view of the child sets the tone for everything else that happens in the classroom.

The invitational environment suggests that infants and toddlers are being invited to participate fully in the life of the classroom and that they are capable of collaborating with the adults in making the space meaningful. Educators can be intentional about this invitation when they consider the aesthetics of the classroom just as they do health and safety guidelines. In *Through a Child's Eyes: How Classroom Design Inspires Learning and Wonder* (Duncan et al., 2018), the authors discuss the natural inclination of early childhood educators to nurture and support young children emotionally, and they advocate for this nurturing disposition to extend to the design of the places that children inhabit.

Focusing on open-ended materials, natural elements, diffused lighting, soft furnishings, and graphics that link children to their culture and community increases the connection that children experience in the classroom environment and to the people within it. Visual display cues, such as picture schedules, photographs showing classroom routines, or documentation of children engaged in investigations, can increase the opportunities for young children to feel connected to the classroom. Including photographs of families as they participate in activities at home or in the community can further the connection between home and school, which is an essential component for learning with infants and toddlers. These displays also can be critical teaching tools in early childhood and an invitation to children and their families to participate in the classroom community.

Early childhood educators often receive mixed messages about what and how materials should be displayed on classroom walls and shelves. Some have had no guidance about what should be included in infant and toddler classroom environments. They may think about what they have seen in other classrooms—even the classrooms of their own early years. Some may have guidance from administrators or co-workers or see ads from commercial vendors in magazines and journals. If early educators have the opportunity to attend conferences, they may see a model classroom set up with beautiful furniture made for specific purposes. In a world where budgets are limited and educators often are not consulted for large expenditures, a connected and inspiring classroom environment may seem unattainable.

Many of us have been influenced by glossy catalogs filled with primary colors, social media posts from other educators, and even the standards meant to guide us. These images can subtly persuade us to buy a product or "decorate" the classroom with matching fabric or splashy bulletin boards. While finding inspiration from the many sources at our fingertips can be beneficial, this also can lead to classrooms that feel institutional and impersonal. Figure 2.2 shows a collection of personal materials that will entice infants to explore.

Children experience space differently than adults. Their experience relies on all their senses. Attending

Figure 2.2. Inviting Areas for Infants to Explore

to the sensory features in a classroom from the perspective of an infant or toddler requires that adults think about aroma, visual elements and lighting, tactile interest, acoustics, the selection of colors, and furniture arrangement—all from a child's-eye view. Early childhood environments that honor children and respect their curiosity and developing competence display features of home and community, reveal elements of complexity that engage their minds and senses, include loose parts and natural materials, and are flexible enough to invite exploration, investigation, and discovery.

THE PHYSICAL ENVIRONMENT: CREATING A PLACE OF WONDER

The physical environment of a classroom has powerful effects on the adults and children who inhabit the space. In his comprehensive book on classroom environments, Jim Greenman (2007) stated, "An environment is a living, changing system" (p. 1). Well-designed environments contribute to the well-being of both the children and adults who share them by inviting children to safely follow their interests and by providing adults time to focus on children's learning. In order to provoke inquiry, infant and toddler educators may need to let go of some previously held beliefs about what should be incorporated into their classroom design and consider the space from a child's point of view. What message is the classroom giving to children?

Infants and toddlers who inhabit classrooms that are poorly designed are likely to hear "no" too frequently. When the environment has too many places that are off-limits or toys and materials that are visible but not available to them, the environment can become educator-directed rather than a place where children can navigate their environment without censure. We once overheard a university student worker tell a new employee that adults were not allowed to say "no" to the children. What the new employee did not yet understand was that the classroom was intentionally designed so that adults did not have to say "no" to children. The environment was saying "yes" to the children's work.

A developmentally designed classroom supports the growth and development of the children and maximizes time for educators to support children by observing, interacting, and facilitating learning. Designing the physical environment for inquiry requires thoughtful consideration of the learning areas and the materials to be included in them. Infant and toddler classrooms require a place for napping and mealtime as well as a space for diapering and toilet training. Once the "must-haves" are in place, it is time to think about how the remaining spaces can be designed with inquiry in mind. In some programs, once these essential items have been placed, there is little real estate left for shelves, tables, and STEM materials. When educators use observation and documentation of children's interests and their understanding of developmental milestones, they can be purposeful when selecting furniture, displays, and learning materials for the classroom.

Educators may want to observe children over several days to determine how they currently are using the space that is available. Thinking through the obstacles with your administrator and team may provide some innovative ways to look at your classroom design. One infant educator in a center where we collaborated placed clear plastic containers filled with materials under each crib so that mobile infants could indicate interest in the materials that were visible. STEM opportunities that could be presented in this way might include those described in Chapters 4–9.

Ask yourself how you can modify your classroom so that time is well spent. Does the environment address children's developing competence? Are there opportunities for children to engage in self-directed learning? Are there places for children to explore interesting materials without interruption? Are there places where they can work with peers and adults? Are there spaces where messy play can take place without impeding the work of others? Can mobile infants and toddlers practice their developing motor skills without interference? Are there any barriers to movement or play that should be addressed? Have you addressed lighting so that each space is illuminated as the play dictates? Is the natural world visible and accessible to children?

Infant and toddler classrooms often are housed in places that originally were not intended for them. Some were designed initially as elementary classrooms or even carved out of industrial or commercial spaces; we know of child care centers constructed over a former swimming pool and a former multiplex theater. A less-than-perfect physical space may limit some options, but with careful consideration of standards for health and safety, the classroom blueprint, the developmental needs of infants and toddlers, and the specific needs of individual children, classrooms can be transformed so that children have opportunities to engage in inquiry-based exploration.

Some experts on classroom design suggest thinking about the balance of the classroom when making decisions about how to organize the space. Duncan and her coauthors (2018) liken classroom design to getting into a canoe. Early educators must think about how to balance the furniture and equipment, as well as the materials and spaces that are used most frequently by the inhabitants. In a classroom that is designed for inquiry, educators plan for exploration, focused play, and cooperation. This may require that the furnishings be reconfigured so that children and adults are not bunched up in the center of the classroom (Greenman, 2007).

Digital cameras or smartphones can be effective tools for determining how the spaces in the classroom are being utilized. Take photos or videos at different times of the day for several successive days. Follow one of the children around the room. Taking the child's perspective might suggest that we get on our hands and knees to survey the world from a child's point of view. Does your perspective about the physical environment change when you are at eye level with a 2-year-old? An infant who is not yet mobile? How do the shelves look when you are observing them from this height? Do they invite exploration? Is it easy to retrieve the materials that you find appealing? Are there enough motivating materials arranged for exploration or are they cluttered and disorganized? Are the displays engaging when viewed at the child's eye level?

Once the classroom has been captured in photos or video, it is time to collaborate with the other adults who share the space. What does the team become aware of when looking at the photos? Does the view from the door invite you to come in and play? Does the classroom make families and visitors feel welcome? Is the environment sufficiently homelike for the infants and toddlers who spend time here? Are there soft spaces for relaxing and cuddling? Are the adults and the children utilizing all of the parts of the classroom that are available to them? How have you addressed the sensory aspects of the environment such as texture, lighting, and natural elements? Are there materials and spaces in the classroom that invite inquiry? Educators who take the child's perspective when designing the classroom space increase opportunities for exploration and engagement with the environment.

Once you have looked at the classroom from the child's point of view, it is time to clear the clutter. Items that are not of interest to the children can be removed and materials that are used only by adults can be stored in a place that is not accessible to the children. Furniture arrangements can be reconfigured so they are flexible and can be shifted quickly to provide additional space for exploration and movement. Lighting should be considered for different parts of the room, making use of natural lighting or nonfluorescent fixtures if possible. Wall and shelf displays should be an invitation for children's learning rather than a distraction.

The educators in this campus-based child care center are ready to welcome the young toddlers to their classroom with labeled cubbies, a place for photos of the children's families placed at eye level, low shelves for displaying appealing materials, and a table for water and sensory exploration. The low tables with chairs are used for mealtimes and for investigating art materials, manipulatives, and loose parts (see Figure 2.3).

There is a housekeeping center in the corner where baby dolls can be cared for, tea parties can be attended, and shoes can be worn—lots of shoes. The carpeted area has a library with soft surroundings for sharing a story with friends, and a rocking chair that easily fits three toddlers with their educator.

Inquiry happens most effectively with a classroom design that allows the adults to respond immediately

Figure 2.3. An Inviting Classroom

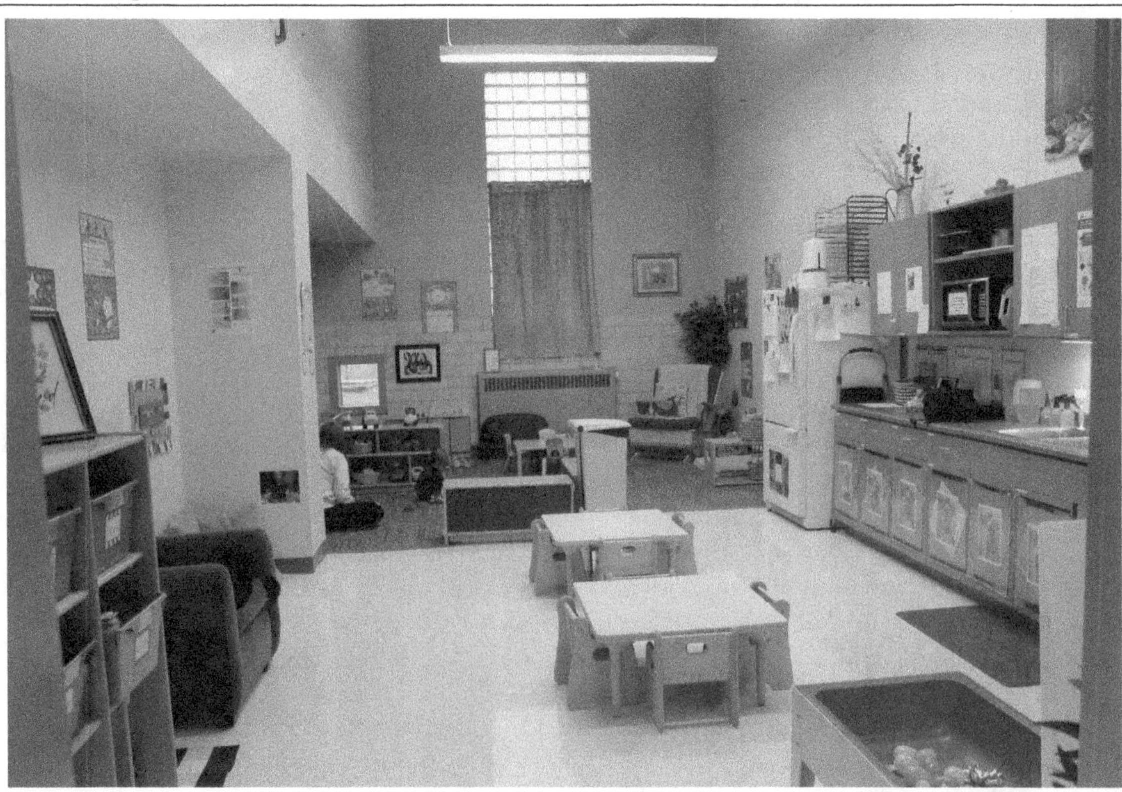

to children's ideas by moving furniture or changing displays to accommodate children's burgeoning interest in an investigation. For instance, when a group of older toddlers began combining the cardboard blocks with the unit blocks during center time, the adults in the classroom were able to move the block shelves against the wall so that the children had more building space. They knew that these toddlers tended to use the blocks directly in front of the shelf unit and that more space would allow them to continue their work. When the children were still occupied with their construction at clean-up time, the educators helped to make a barrier so that their building could be continued later. The addition of labels to identify the builders and a directive to "save my work" can give children permission to continue their building endeavors at the next opportunity.

All children need a place where they are encouraged and invited to explore and try out their ideas. For infants and toddlers, the environment must be planned with the understanding that mobile infants and toddlers will investigate everything! When educators design a classroom from the point of view of the children rather than from the adults' perspective, infants and toddlers will be invited to engage with the space and the materials in new and interesting ways. Thoughtfully designed infant and toddler spaces say "yes—you can move that," "you can play here," "that was placed there just for you!" Engaging environments contribute to learning in much the same way as the materials selected. Providing infants and toddlers with inviting places, interesting materials, and ample time to investigate them without interference, rather than planning specific one-and-done activities, builds inquiry into the environment.

THE INTELLECTUAL ENVIRONMENT: CREATING A PLACE WHERE LEARNING HAPPENS

We now know that the cognitive abilities of young children far surpass what previously has been attributed to them. Research from the past 30 years has illuminated the importance of relationships with trusting adults and early experiences that take into account the competencies as well as the vulnerabilities of infants and toddlers. Early on they are able to imagine another person's experiences, understand cause and effect, and begin to construct ideas and theories about how things work in the world (Gopnik, 2010). This awareness about how infants and toddlers learn, and the importance of early experiences, is the basis for the Infant Toddler Inquiry Learning Model.

A child's thinking and learning are guided by responsive caregiving. Adults who are intentional in each interaction with a child can support inquiry learning by providing experiences that encourage increased engagement and support the development of new understanding. When adults maximize opportunities for back-and-forth exchanges with young children, inquiry learning opportunities can be embedded in experiences throughout the day. While we certainly encourage careful planning for STEM experiences, we also acknowledge that unplanned opportunities often can be the learning experiences with the greatest impact.

We recall an experience that occurred in a classroom where we were collaborating with an educator of older toddlers. Two of the children in the classroom were playing with some plastic dishes in the housekeeping area. One of them found a metal washer and began to drop it onto one of the plates. They listened to the sound that the washer made as it hit the plate and then dropped the washer on another plate that was topped with some plastic lettuce. Their educator was observing and documenting their work and noticed that when the washer was dropped on the plate with the plastic lettuce, the sound was softened or muffled, but when the washer landed on the empty plate the sound was not muffled. The educator intentionally asked an action question (Martens, 1999): "What happens if you take the [plastic] food from the plate? Does it change the sound if you take the food from the plate?" One of the children removed all the food, and the other one dropped the washer, which made a loud sound as it hit the plate. The other child voluntarily added a piece of plastic food to the plate and listened to the sound that was made when the washer was dropped again. The children continued to drop pieces of plastic food on top of the one previously added. Each time, they dropped the washer on the top and then listened for the sound variation. The educator was observing and documenting their play and noticed their wonder as they used new strategies with materials they had used previously. Their delight in their newfound discovery encouraged them to create more sounds with the materials as they tried out new strategies for making something interesting happen. Their educator recognized that they were engaged in this inquiry and supported their problem solving by noticing what they were doing and scaffolding the experience with comments and questions.

They communicated their delight in the educator's interest of their discovery when she encouraged their continuation of this sound experience. She documented their learning by videotaping, taking photographs, and transcribing their conversation about what they were doing. This in-the-moment inquiry learning opportunity was not planned, but it was a powerful serve-and-return interaction between the adult and the young children because the educator was observant and took advantage of an opportunity.

In our work with infant and toddler educators, we see many classroom STEM opportunities that are not being recognized as such. When young children pour and measure at the water center, "cook" in the mud kitchen, mix paint at the easel, or build ramps for their large-wheeled toys on the playground, they are engaging in science, technology, engineering, and math. When educators recognize the STEM opportunities embedded in experiences that have been part of early childhood classrooms for decades, they have the opportunity to engage children at deeper levels by noticing their wonder, documenting the old and new strategies they use, and commenting or questioning in order to understand the children's resolution of the problems they have posed for themselves.

In inquiry learning environments, adults provide opportunities for infants and toddlers to engage in experiences that encourage problem solving, curiosity, question formation, and exploring the world around them. Children's engagement in inquiry learning experiences supports their desire to understand their world. Teachable moments are not opportunities to give the child the "right answer," but instead are moments in which the educator observes a child and provides the right amount of support so that the child can follow their own interests and solve the problem they have posed for themselves. While it is essential for educators to plan the environment, select materials carefully, and manage the daily schedule with intent, it is equally important that we follow the child's lead in our interactions during play routines.

Providing an environment where learning happens for infants and toddlers means putting aside the idea that programs for our youngest children should focus on meeting particular goals and objectives set out by the adults with narrowly focused "lessons" that mirror preschool or early elementary programs. Infants and toddlers learn differently than school-aged children, and the experiences we plan for them must consider this understanding. Using a reflective curriculum process (Lally, 2009) suggests planning the environment carefully and providing rich and open-ended experiences rather than developing specific lessons or activities. Reflective planning requires developing a deep understanding of each child's unique interests and skills by observing and documenting carefully, and supporting the work that each child is already doing. By demonstrating respect for what young children know and can do, we increase the chances for them to gain confidence and competence.

Infants and toddlers engage in inquiry as they use interesting materials to produce an effect that creates a question, a desire to answer this question, and the confidence to move forward with their investigation. Experiences that allow children to make something happen (producible); to cause the action to occur right away (immediate); to see, hear, or feel what happens (observable); and to have the ability to change something and try again (variable) provide worthwhile STEM learning for infants and toddlers (Kamii & DeVries, 1993).

VALERIE AND THE INFANT TODDLER INQUIRY LEARNING MODEL

In this example from a young toddler classroom, Valerie explored the light pad and the loose parts that were available for her investigation. She used familiar strategies to explore the physical properties of the translucent, transparent, and opaque objects. She noticed the pebbles in the basket and began to arrange them around the edge of the light table. She did not dump or drop them, but chose particular pebbles and created a design that she found appealing. She continued to move the materials around the light table and then paused to observe the results of her work. She modified the array of materials so that they fit on the light pad and provided an attractive visual display.

TEXTBOX 2.2. VALERIE EXPLORES THE LIGHT PAD

Valerie (22 months) joined her educator at the child-sized table where a light pad and variety of materials had been set up for investigation. Valerie selected some translucent multicolored pebbles and began to place them on the edges of the light pad. She moved them around in several different configurations, pausing to observe the results. When she had explored these materials for several minutes, she looked through the basket and selected some translucent nesting cups. She placed them on the light pad and dropped some of the pebbles into the cups and looked at them. She poured out the pebbles and then nested the cups. She next discovered the child-sized flashlights and placed two of them on the light table. She moved them into her display of pebbles and cups. She remained at the light pad for 15 minutes trying a variety of materials in several combinations. The educator remained sitting near her. Valerie remained focused on her work as other children selected materials from the shared array and moved in and out of the area (see Figure 2.4).

Valerie then selected the translucent nesting cups from the basket of materials. She looked at the pebbles she had placed on the light table and began to drop some of the pebbles into the cups she had chosen. She tried out old strategies and then combined them with new strategies when she closely regarded the pebbles from the top of the cup and then through the side by picking up the cup and placing it at eye level. When she had looked at several of the cups filled with pebbles, she dumped them all out and began to nest the cups. She used a familiar strategy to place them inside one another, paying close attention to the way they fit. She attempted to place one of the large cups inside a smaller cup, observed the results, then removed it to change the order of the cups so they would nest. She attended

Figure 2.4. Valerie Explores Light

to the size and shape of the individual materials, the position of the pebbles on the light pad in relation to one another, and the volume of the cups or how many pebbles each could hold.

Valerie demonstrated her satisfaction with the exploration and the actions she had taken by accepting solutions to several problems and by repeating the actions that were successful. At several points in her investigation, she looked at the educator who was near her and smiled but did not indicate that she required assistance or that she needed additional materials.

EQUITY IN INFANT AND TODDLER INQUIRY LEARNING ENVIRONMENTS

Inquiry learning opportunities in infant and toddler classrooms must be accessible to every child every day. "All children have the right to equitable learning opportunities that help them achieve their full potential as engaged learners and valued members of society" (National Association for the Education of Young Children [NAEYC], 2019, p. 1). Early childhood educators working in infant and toddler classrooms provide an introduction to the larger educational community for many children and families. It is imperative that as the first representatives of this community, infant and toddler educators provide support for access to participation in learning opportunities and social interactions for all infants and toddlers regardless of race, culture, class, gender, ability or disability, religion, or any other identities.

This begins with an understanding of what is developmentally appropriate for children in this age group, what standards have been established for children in the setting, and what supports or modifications can be provided to make inquiry learning possible for all children. Universal Design for Learning (CAST, 2018) is a research-based framework that provides guidelines for decreasing the barriers and challenges and increasing the flexibility in learning environments so that all children have access to age-appropriate settings, materials, and instruction. UDL describes three networks that must be addressed when planning for learning. Infants and toddlers need access to multiple means of engagement, multiple means of representation, and multiple means of action and expression.

Educators can provide access to learning by developing an understanding of how each child in their setting attends to the materials and people in the classroom and then offering authentic experiences that connect children to what is important to them. Offering children choices, providing opportunities to work and play independently, eliminating barriers to play, and creating predictable routines can help to ensure that all children are fully engaged.

Educators who present materials and information with multiple approaches can assist all children to access learning opportunities. Using gestures, sign language, picture symbols, or key phrases in a child's home language can increase the likelihood of comprehension. Introducing simple songs that emphasize routines, posting simple picture schedules depicting classroom procedures, and using prompts or scaffolds are all helpful tools for an early childhood educator.

By using low-tech tools such as picture schedules or object schedules, making simple adaptations to materials, or purchasing toys and equipment that have built-in access, such as knobbed puzzles or indestructible books that are made for hands-on reading, educators can assist children to participate in experiences and to express what they know and understand. Daily communication with families also can keep the educator informed about what each child is doing at home and what is needed for success.

Infants and toddlers learn best in an environment that is culturally, linguistically, and developmentally suited for them and builds on their strengths and the strengths of their families. Educators who serve these young learners must provide the supports that are needed in order to access the curriculum, navigate the environment, and communicate with others. To offer these learning opportunities, educators and families require access to professional development and community resources that will assist them to develop the knowledge, skills, and dispositions necessary to successfully implement equitable learning environments for all infants and toddlers.

PUTTING IT ALL TOGETHER

Designing an inquiry learning environment for infants and toddlers must be intentional and based on observation, documentation, and consideration of each aspect of the environment. With an ongoing reflective process, educators can achieve the delicate balance between safety and an invitation to explore independently. When infant and toddler educators understand how the environment can support inquiry learning, their natural instincts for selecting and providing high-quality early learning experiences will be enhanced and refined. As children acquire new skills and interests, move into the classroom, or move on to new classrooms, educators can modify the environment to accommodate these changes. Educators of these youngest children can support the learning of each and every child by creating spaces filled with a variety of intriguing materials, flexible furnishings, effectively placed lighting, thoughtfully designed displays, and responsive adults with an understanding of the importance of relationships for learning.

When infant and toddler educators understand what is needed for an inquiry learning environment and what STEM means for young children, many will find that they are already providing science, technology, engineering, and math in their daily activities. With some consideration of the language used to scaffold these activities, reorganizing of the classroom space, increased scrutiny of the visual displays, and the addition of some recycled or inexpensive materials, educators can turn classroom activities into inquiry learning experiences that infants and toddlers will return to again and again.

Observation, Documentation, and Assessment: The Educator's Role in Infant and Toddler Inquiry

Sonia Yoshizawa, Sherri Peterson, and Jill Uhlenberg

Chapter 3 will focus on you, the educator. In previous chapters, we have described the importance of inquiry learning and teaching, and how supporting children through inquiry empowers them to be future thinkers and lifelong learners.

We introduced the Infant Toddler Inquiry Learning Model, a nonlinear model indicating how young children may process their thinking as they explore and engage with materials. Chapter 2 describes the environment that serves as a learning and teaching platform that supports children by optimizing their learning as they safely wonder, strategize, and resolve with experiences that interest them and spark their curiosity.

Learning is a journey and so is teaching. Whether the child you are caring for is a 6-month-old who is not yet mobile or an active toddler who loves to giggle and bounce while inventing a silly song, your verbal and nonverbal interactions are sending signals to the child constantly. Children observe your behavior through your expressions and reactions, and interpret whether you are responding positively or negatively to them. A true and open interest in children's budding inquiry skills establishes the foundation of security, so that they feel safe to proceed with their exploration and investigation, and more important, signals your invitation to repeat their actions and make mistakes.

Your role as an educator is to respond thoughtfully to their signals, value their interests, support their curiosity, and extend their capacity, whether their actions translate to: "Let me try it on my own," or "I need help." As they explore the materials for the first time or for the 50th time, your response to them

can boost competence, autonomy, and perseverance, all necessary in the development of lifelong learners who feel secure as they find problems and work out the solutions to those problems. "Teachers can create and carry out a classroom culture that either fosters or discourages engaged and active thinkers" (Salmon & Barrera, 2021, p. 60).

THE EDUCATOR'S ROLE: NURTURING YOUR PERSPECTIVE-TAKING SKILLS

An essential practice that we recommend for early childhood educators is to mess about with materials (Hawkins, 1965) before they are introduced to children. Some educators look at us in surprise when we suggest that they play, especially with materials that are designed for infants and toddlers. It is easy to imagine that we understand all the possibilities for such familiar objects as plastic containers with lids, squishy balls, nesting cups, and clear tubes. In our experience, it is essential to try them out so that we can understand fully what infants and toddlers might do with them. The experience will be enhanced for children when adults contemplate the possibilities in the properties of the materials, the way the materials can be combined to produce an interesting effect, and what children might or might not be able to do with them. When we have included this practice in our own professional learning sessions, we have observed educators who were engaging in the same processes that infants and toddlers used, as they explored the STEM materials introduced in their classrooms.

Jamie was an intentional educator. She prepared simple variations of common activities to pique the toddlers' interest and engage them in both finding and solving problems through their experiences. Jamie set up this paint table often, varying the kind of paper she used so the toddlers could explore how the paint and paper interacted. She also chose this activity in addition to using the easel because of the different ways the paint responded on this horizontal surface compared with the upright easel (see Figure 3.1).

Figure 3.1. Eric Makes a Hole

> ### Textbox 3.1. Painting the Table
>
> Jamie prepared a paint table in the toddler room by taping sheets of construction paper on a table until the entire surface was covered. As she completed the task, Eric put on a paint smock and came to the table. Chloe joined him but left quickly to explore the block center. Eric waited patiently as Jamie set paint cups and brushes on the edge of the table. He looked at Jamie, who nodded that he could begin to paint. Jamie continued to prepare other art materials nearby.
>
> Eric began by painting a small circle near the edge of the table. He stopped each time he refilled his paintbrush, looking at the painted spot for a moment. After a short time, the construction paper began to dissolve away so that Eric was painting the tabletop where the paper had disintegrated. Jamie observed this process quietly. Eric was so engaged that he did not speak to Jamie, and Jamie did not intervene. Eric continued to paint, review his work, and refill his brush as the painted area in the paper slowly grew to an 8-inch hole. After a final inspection, Eric put down the brush, removed his smock, and joined others in the pretend play center.

Jamie had used the strategy of selective intervention because she saw that Eric was deeply engaged in his painting process. She had not anticipated Eric's actions with the paint and paper but saw no reason to stop him from exploring. Jamie stayed nearby, ready to give Eric encouragement or support if he became upset with the process or spoke to Jamie about the hole in the paper. In her approach to classroom management, she tried to be flexible and open to the toddlers' ideas, adding new materials when interest slowed.

THE EDUCATOR'S ROLE: OBSERVATION

Effective educators use observations to make decisions about the social–emotional, physical, invitational, and intellectual environments. A responsive curriculum that takes into account the interests and needs of each and every child is dependent on judicious use of observations paired with reflection and collaboration with other educators who have observed and considered the implications of what children are doing. Observation is a way to better understand children by watching them carefully (Jablon et al., 2007).

Observation in infant and toddler classrooms is the basis for decisions that are made about every aspect of the classroom environment. As we observe children's actions and consider the meaning of those actions, we gain a window into the children's thinking and possible theories (Foreman & Hall, 2005). With older children, we can listen to their conversations and ponder their questions so that we are better able to understand possible goals and strategies. Infants and toddlers may not yet be able to verbalize the questions that they have in mind when trying to understand how the world works (Greenfield et al., 2017).

Observations can direct us to an understanding of the purpose of their questions. We may discern those questions when children demonstrate resolve with selected problems, or we may never understand the questions they are posing. With infants and toddlers, our observations must rely to a great degree on their actions with the materials. These actions are informed by our relationships with individual children and our knowledge of typical development in general as well as what is characteristic for an individual child.

Mariel explored a collection of containers with lids. She seemed most interested in a large container with a screw-on lid that held a variety of small toys (see Figure 3.2).

> ### TEXTBOX 3.2. MARIEL DISCOVERS A PLASTIC JAR AND LID
>
> Mariel sat near the shelves in her toddler classroom. A basket with a variety of containers was on the lowest shelf. Mariel reached and tipped it so that she could pick up one of the small containers. She attempted to remove the lid. Olivia, one of the classroom staff, was sitting nearby. When Mariel was unable to remove the lid from the plastic jar, she looked at Olivia and squealed to indicate her need for assistance. Olivia interrupted her squealing to say, "Help, please," and accompanied the words with the sign for help. She repeated the direction when Mariel continued to squeal, demonstrated removing the lid, then handed it to Mariel, who tried again.
>
> Mariel's friend came to the same area and tipped the materials from the basket onto the floor. Mariel continued to investigate items from the basket and floor. She tried again to open the jar by turning the lid. When she was successful, she held up the jar and lid and looked toward Olivia. When Olivia and another educator continued working with other children, Mariel put her mouth on the jar. She blew into it to produce a sound and looked up again. She grinned and put the lid on, then took it off and used it to make more sounds. She repeated her action several times

and then replaced the lid. Mariel opened the jar again, put her mouth on it, and produced a unique sound. She made eye contact with Olivia and repeated her action. She then tried the same strategy with the lid and produced another sound. She went back and forth between the lid and the jar several times and then stopped to try to get the lid on the jar. Mariel placed her mouth on the jar once again and then dropped it on the floor. She retrieved the lid and placed her mouth on it and continued to make sounds. Olivia looked up and said to her, "Do you like that sound, Mariel?" Mariel continued the noise-making for some time and looked around to see whether others had noticed her jar concert.

Figure 3.2. Mariel Tries to Open the Lid

In this example from a young toddler classroom, we saw Olivia observe Mariel's determination to open the jar, support her by noticing her efforts and providing language and modeling, and extend her learning by acknowledging her innovation when she found a way to make sounds with the jar after opening it. Adults play a critical role as children begin to explore and make sense of their world (McClure et al., 2017). Observation and documentation during the inquiry learning process are critical for educators to determine how they can give just the right amount of support to infants and toddlers as they engage in inquiry. Supportive adult–child relationships foster children's developing confidence in their ability to figure things out. When infants and toddlers are engaged in a caring relationship with adults who provide them with multiple opportunities to use inspiring materials, their budding competence as investigators can be facilitated.

In this classroom, educators engaged the learners by using their observations to identify and stimulate interest and capitalize on children's natural curiosity. The young toddlers in this classroom had been investigating the materials in the housekeeping corner by emptying and filling the recycled materials found on the shelves. The educators noticed the children's delight in a particular type of jar that looked like translucent glass but was made of a safe material. The jar had a gold lid that was easy to turn and was just the right size to fit in a toddler hand. They found several of these jars with the recycled materials and added them to woven baskets near the block corner. Additional containers were placed on the shelves around the classroom so that the children had more opportunities to dump, fill, transport, transform, connect, and disconnect interesting objects.

Olivia facilitated Mariel's exploration of the materials when she observed Mariel's frustration with her unsuccessful efforts to remove the lid from the jar and then supported Mariel's problem solving by demonstrating a way to remove the lid. She fostered communication when she said, "Help, please," and added the sign for help. She then handed the jar to Mariel so that she could continue her efforts to solve the problem of removing the lid from the jar.

Young children need encouragement for their innovations rather than praise for what adults deem success. In our work with infants and toddlers and their educators, we have observed the inquiry learning process unfold when children are inspired to use materials in their own way and in their own time as educators observe, document learning, and use this information to plan for further STEM experiences. In her book *The Power of Emergent Curriculum*, Carol Anne Wien (2014) discussed the importance of unhurried time in early childhood classrooms. She suggested that educators alter the lens by which they observe children in order to be attentive to the connections children are making in relation to their environment, that they hesitate before stepping in so that children have the opportunity to take action, and that they study their documentation in order to see and understand the things they had not noticed before.

In this unplanned moment with Mariel in her classroom, we saw an educator supporting a young toddler as she initiated an experience and followed her interest. The educator provided support and encouragement for Mariel to be an active participant in her own learning. Effective early childhood educators realize that it is important to find the right tool at the right time (National Research Council, 2001), using both educator-guided experiences and child-initiated experiences that engage children and encourage them to be active participants in their learning. Effective educators find opportunities to support learning in both child-guided and educator-guided experiences. This interconnectedness between adults and children is an essential component of curriculum in an inquiry-based infant and toddler program.

We are reminded of our own journey to a more inquiry-based model of learning and teaching. One of us was being observed in her early childhood classroom as part of an educator inquiry group of which she was a member. Her classroom was inclusive and had children with a wide variety of needs. One 3-year-old, Daniel, was experiencing episodes of severe behavior that included noncompliance, inappropriate language, and serious aggression. This behavior sometimes was escalated when the routine was disrupted or when visitors arrived.

One part of the observation was large-group time, where this educator was introducing materials for exploring sound. Her agenda was written clearly in her lesson plans, with objectives identified for individual children in compliance with their individual education plans (IEPs). During the lesson, Daniel interrupted with an idea for how he could make sound with the materials that the educator had introduced. He jumped up and moved to the center of the circle where the materials were located and began to pound on one of the cans with a striker. He was asked to sit and wait for his turn. He did sit but was clearly unhappy that he was not allowed to share his idea. After the children left for the day, a mentor/coach asked during the discussion, "What do you think might have happened if Daniel had gotten to share his idea?" Certainly, a simple enough question, but for this educator it was a very important moment in her shift to a more child-centered model of learning and teaching. Although it has been nearly 25 years since that day, it is still a reminder about how important it is to examine our practice to determine what we could shift in order to support the young children in our lives. What would have happened if Daniel had shared his idea? As we have learned, young children often have ideas we never would have thought of, and they use materials in innovative ways.

THE EDUCATOR'S ROLE: DOCUMENTATION FOR PLANNING

Educators can make decisions about learning when they observe children to determine what they know and can do, and reflect on their observations (see Figure 3.3). This supports planning for experiences that will be meaningful. Documentation for planning in an inquiry-based infant and toddler program includes insights into adult–child interactions, relationships developing among children, children's actions with materials, and evidence of the impact that the indoor and outdoor environment has on learning. When effective documentation follows observation, the research in which children are engaged during investigations can be revealed so that planning for further learning can be addressed. "The infant-toddler teacher does not start planning the curriculum with a list of activities, but rather starts planning for the day or week by observing what the children are doing and learning in all developmental domains" (Wittmer & Petersen, 2018, p. 319). Documentation of children's actions also must include reflection and conversation among educators

Figure 3.3. Sherri Documents Children's Actions

so that meaning can be made of what is being observed. This requires that program administrators provide dedicated time for educator collaboration in order to design high-quality curriculum that supports the needs of infants and toddlers.

Documentation can take many forms, including photos, videos, checklists, or anecdotal records, to name a few. One system that has worked well for educators with whom we have collaborated is to use a steno pad and make a heading on each side for notes (see Figure 3.4).

On the left-hand side write "what the child is doing" and on the right-hand side, "what this might mean." This approach can be used during STEM investigations and during daily routines to document children's actions and the educator's consideration of the meaning of those actions, with the understanding that our thoughts about children's motives may be inaccurate.

What are some other effective ways to document what infants and toddlers are accomplishing? You may have developed your own methods for documenting what infants and toddlers know and can do. We have listed a few that we have used or have observed in classrooms where we spend time with educators and young children, and some thoughts on organizing them.

Figure 3.4. Stenographer's Pad for Recording Observations

What the child is doing	What this might mean
Mariel is holding a small jar in her hands and trying to turn the lid	Mariel held the jar in one hand and turned the lid with the other hand
Mariel looked at Olivia & squealed	Mariel wants Olivia to notice her and help her remove the lid
Olivia demonstrated how to turn the lid and Mariel grabbed it to try again	Olivia gave the jar to Mariel who tried for several minutes to turn the lid until it was removed.
Mariel tried to turn the lid and got it off – then looked over at Olivia	Mariel wants Olivia to see what she has accomplished

- Digital camera for photos and video—make time to download and organize into files for individual children or by date
- Notes function on phone or app that is voice-to-text
- Sticky notes and pen kept in a pocket for on-the-spot documentation
- Work samples such as art projects or beginning writing samples, which also can be photographed so that storage is not a problem
- Clipboard with a place for notes listing the date and observations of children
- Steno pad with headings for each column
- A dedicated place to file these observations so that they are easily accessed
- A plan for documentation (one educator we know had a weekly schedule for each of the adults assigned to the classroom so that each child was observed weekly by at least two people)

THE EDUCATOR'S ROLE: ASSESSMENT

Infant and toddler educators become experts on the young children they support. Daily interactions that include such essential routines as feeding, diapering, and comforting give insight into the developmental progress, temperaments, wants, and needs of the children who are in their care. These daily interactions, accompanied by observation and documentation, strengthen the relationships formed in infant and toddler classrooms. In addition, these observations inform educators as they discover the individual approaches to learning and dispositions of infants and toddlers. But how do educators know that all children are thriving in the learning environment they have created?

The 2020 National Association for the Education of Young Children *Position Statement on Developmentally Appropriate Practice* states:

> Observing, documenting, and assessing each child's development and learning are essential processes for educators and programs to plan, implement, and evaluate the effectiveness of the experiences they provide to children. Assessment includes both formal and informal measures as tools for monitoring children's progress toward a program's desired goals. (p. 19)

Assessment of infants and toddlers can appear to be a daunting task when we consider the reality of the classroom educator whose days are filled with caregiving routines for young children with individual needs. However, assessment is a critical task for educators and should be part of any high-quality early childhood program so that documentation can be gathered about a child's performance over time. This allows educators to communicate with families about their child's growth and development and provides information for planning an appropriate curriculum for all children. In order for assessment to be valuable, educators require training that addresses the following:

- The impact relationships have on learning
- Typical developmental milestones
- Program standards and assessment expectations

- Techniques for communicating effectively with families
- The how of assessment, including training for technology that facilitates efficient documentation and planning

Educators' documentation of children is essential to identifying strengths and assessing development (NAEYC, 2019).

Forms of Assessment

Assessment can take a variety of forms and can be either program-developed child assessment tools that are created by educators or administrators to align with the program's philosophy or curriculum, or published child assessment tools that have been researched and are considered a reliable source for reporting on a child's development. There are published assessments available that rely on observations of children in natural play settings and daily routines, those that include portfolios with photographs and examples of children's work along with educator documentation, rating scales that are completed by parents or by educators, and standardized tests that sometimes are used to determine eligibility for particular services. Some programs may use different assessment methods for different purposes.

Programs vary widely in the expectations they have for educators regarding assessment. In some publicly funded programs such as Head Start, children are screened in both developmental domain expectations and social–emotional development. Educators look at scores to determine which children currently are not meeting developmental expectations and then re-screen them after they have had time to adjust to the classroom routine and develop trusting relationships with educators. Families complete a questionnaire to identify social–emotional strengths and risk factors, and educators use this information as they plan programming.

The Head Start Early Learning Outcomes Framework (ELOF; U.S. Department of Health and Human Services, Administration on Children, Youth and Families/Office of Head Start, 2015) and individual state standards are used to provide guidance to educators about the continuum of learning for children birth to 5. Educators are required to implement program and teaching practices that are aligned with the ELOF. Specific tools for assessment of individual student progress vary from program to program. In many of the classrooms where we have collaborated, educators use *Teaching Strategies GOLD* (Heroman et al., 2010) or the HighScope Child Observation Record—*COR Advantage* (HighScope Educational Research Foundation, 2015), which both are aligned with state standards and describe what children should know and be able to do. Curriculum materials accompany both of these assessment tools, but many programs are not required to use those specific materials even if they are using the assessment instrument.

Many programs have far fewer guidelines for observing, documenting, and assessing infants and toddlers. Some have no guidelines for educators regarding how children's progress is monitored, although most child care programs expect educators to communicate with families of infants and toddlers about daily routines such as sleep schedules, diapering, feeding, and temperament. Increasingly, programs are using technology for this communication, such as an application that can be shared reciprocally. Some applications have the option of monitoring developmental milestones as well as daily communication, or include scope and sequence information, so families are informed about expected developmental milestones.

So how do you determine what is right for your program? In Figure 3.5, we compare some common tools—state standards (Iowa Early Learning Standards, 3rd ed. [Iowa Department of Education, 2018]), a curricular framework (Head Start Early Learning Outcomes Framework, known as ELOF), and two commercial assessment tools (*Teaching Strategies GOLD* and *COR Advantage*)—to determine what they might have in common. There are many commonalities in the domains that are included, and educators may be guided by their program and funding source as they select the system that is the best fit for them.

Purposes of Assessment

The information obtained during inquiry learning opportunities and daily routines can set children up for success when educators use their observations

Figure 3.5. Common Early Childhood Assessment Tools

Domains	Early Learning Standards	Head Start ELOF	Teaching Strategies GOLD	HighScope COR Advantage
Social–Emotional Development	X	X	X	X
Physical Development, Motor Skills, Health	X	X	X	X
Approaches to Learning	X	X		X
Cognition		X	X	
Language, Literacy, Communication	X	X	X	X
Mathematics	X		X	X
Science, Technology	X		X	X
Social Studies	X		X	
Creative Arts	X		X	X
English Language Learning			X	X

to learn more about individual children, track their progress, and make decisions about learning opportunities that they will offer. The Inquiry Teaching Model guides educators to start with observation. To engage learners, provide opportunities, and make program decisions that will stimulate interest and capitalize on children's natural curiosity, educators rely on observations of children. When educators make observation and documentation a part of every day, they will be able provide opportunities for young children that support problem solving and their developing language and communication skills. Observation is not assessment, but rather a method that can be used in assessment (Bell, 2017). Close observation will enable educators to find out what children know and can do, and determine what areas need further development. Learning is integrated for infants and toddlers, so these domains serve primarily as a way to organize the scope of the curriculum. A single learning experience often supports children's development across multiple domains. In the example with Mariel and her jar, we see how even an unplanned opportunity can provide insight into her learning in several domain areas. This is demonstrated in Figure 3.6.

Implementing an assessment system is the responsibility of the infant or toddler educator. When you have selected a tool or procedure for documenting children's learning, you have made a commitment to improving the quality of the experience for the children you serve. Assessment should be ongoing and should occur during a variety of experiences over time. It is a cycle that includes providing opportunities, observing and documenting during those experiences, reflecting on the documentation, communicating with other educators about your reflections and to families about their child, and analyzing and evaluating the information in order to provide more opportunities based on the new information. In our view, an inquiry learning environment includes all these elements in order to best meet the needs of children.

THE EDUCATOR'S ROLE: MAKING LEARNING VISIBLE

Making learning visible (Rinaldi, 1994) is a hallmark of Reggio Emilia classrooms and an idea that has been adopted by many early childhood programs. When you make learning visible to the children, their families, the community you serve, and other early childhood educators, you are elevating the work you are doing and proclaiming to others that what infants and toddlers know and can do is worth shouting about. So, what do we mean by making learning visible and how do we execute a plan for communicating to others about the work we are doing while completing our daily routines? You may already have a plan in place for recording your observations and reporting to parents. We add some tips we have used or observed.

At the beginning of the year, as you welcome families to your classroom, make sure that you have

Figure 3.6. Observation and Assessment

What the Child Is Doing	What This Might Mean	Domains That Could Be Addressed
Mariel is holding a small jar in her hands and trying to turn the lid.	Mariel is demonstrating fine-motor control as she holds the jar and tries to remove the lid by turning it.	Motor skills, approaches to learning, cognition
Mariel looks at the educator and squeals.	Mariel is asking the educator to help her. She may want the educator to remove the lid for her, or she may want the educator to show her how to remove the lid.	Communication, social–emotional development, approaches to learning, cognition
After the educator shows Mariel how to remove the lid by turning, she tries again to remove the lid from the jar by using the new strategy.	Mariel uses the new strategy until the lid has been removed. She spends several minutes turning the lid until she is successful.	Motor skills, approaches to learning, cognition, science
Mariel is successful and she looks at Olivia.	Mariel wants Olivia to notice her and what she has accomplished.	Communication, social–emotional development
Mariel puts her mouth on the jar and blows into the jar to make a sound.	Mariel wants the educator to notice her. She uses a new strategy to get Olivia's attention.	Communication, social–emotional development, approaches to learning, science
Mariel picks up the lid and blows into it.	Mariel has identified a new problem. What happens when I blow into the lid rather than the jar? Does she want Olivia's attention, or has her focus moved to the sounds she is creating?	Communication, social–emotional development, science, cognition, approaches to learning
Mariel goes back and forth between lid and jar, making sounds with each.	Mariel is investigating the physics of sound by trying old strategies and developing new strategies with the materials. She is focused on the problem rather than attention from Olivia.	Science, cognition, approaches to learning
Mariel makes a new sound when she adds spit to the jar.	Mariel is interested in the sounds she is producing. She also wants the educator to notice her efforts and the sounds she is producing. When Mariel's efforts do not get the results she wants, she adds a new material and develops a new strategy.	Communication, social–emotional development, science, cognition, approaches to learning

written permission to take photos and videotape children. Explaining the purpose of documenting children's work will alleviate parental concerns about how photos will be used and shared. If you are using a digital camera or an app to document your observations, you may already have the content that you need in order to begin making the learning in your classroom visible. If you are compiling portfolios as part of your assessment system, using a parent communication app, or a web-based assessment tool, you may already be gathering artifacts that can be used for communicating children's thinking and learning.

Displays may include artifacts from open-ended art experiences, beginning writing samples from older toddlers, language samples, or photos of the children engaged in play for learning. Photos should be accompanied by documentation that describes what the children were doing and what that might mean, or standards that were addressed during the experience. Families will be interested in seeing how many learning objectives can be met while children are engaged in child-initiated play or in daily routines in the classroom. Visitors to your program will come away from the visual displays with new understanding about the meaning in children's play and the importance of rich experiences for infants and toddlers (see Figure 3.7). Our profession will be elevated by this new understanding about how much you, as an early childhood educator, contribute to the health and well-being of the children in your care and how much you know about child development.

Figure 3.7. Display of Children's Learning

Visual displays may consist of documentation panels that tell the story of a field trip, project, or the work that was done in a STEM center. In one center, educators developed a hallway display that contained photos of all children in the classroom engaged in a developmental physical knowledge experience called Chutes and Silos (see Chapter 6). The display included photos of the children, documentation from observations by educators, examples of standards being met in the center, and some of the materials used during the investigation.

Visual displays also can include learning stories about individual children, with your documentation about the child's actions and what they might mean. Families can contribute to the stories with observations gleaned from their own activities, routines, or outings. Documentation of progress over time in the same or a similar activity can demonstrate how the curriculum is helping to shape outcomes for the children in the program.

Visual displays also can be developed for infants and toddlers so they can see themselves on the walls around the room. Laminating the documentation and displaying it at the children's level allows them

to see the photos that demonstrate their developing competence. In one program where we spend time, photos of the children and their families engaged in familiar routines were displayed on the cupboard doors and the front of the refrigerator. Children were encouraged to remove them while educators engaged them in conversation about whom they were interacting with and what they were doing in the photo. In another classroom, the educator made a home visit at the beginning of the year and took a photo of each child with their family in front of their home. The photos were inserted into a Word document with the child's name, printed, laminated, and bound for a class book. The book was a favorite of the infants and toddlers throughout the school year and provided conversation starters and comfort on difficult days.

Communicating about the work you are doing with infants and toddlers is an essential part of the inquiry process. Visual displays can assist in the reflection and planning process, enable you to communicate with families and visitors about the importance of what children are doing, and engage children in their own thinking about the experiences you provide. If you are new to the idea of using documentation in this way, we urge you to try it. You can implement some of the ideas and use your colleagues as sounding boards as you reflect on how to make learning visible in your program. We think it will transform your practice and change the way you think about your work.

THE EDUCATOR'S ROLE: REFLECTIVE PRACTICE FOR MAKING DECISIONS

Reflective practice is the art of stepping back to consider what you have observed and documented. It requires that you think about, examine, and question your assumptions about what children are doing. Collaborating with other educators elevates the experience as you listen to one another's perspectives on what you have documented. You are acting as researchers and child development specialists as you dig deeper into what you know about the infants and toddlers in your classrooms. In your work with other educators, you have the opportunity to share observations about children's ideas and actions, reflect on what you have noticed in order to discern children's interests and questions, and create learning opportunities that are informed by your observations about the children in your care. Reflective practice is a hallmark of high-quality learning and teaching. You and the children you care for deserve the time it takes to share your observations and insights with other professionals in order to ensure the best outcomes for children and families.

THE EDUCATOR'S ROLE: DOCUMENTING CHILDREN'S LEARNING FOR REFLECTIVE PRACTICE

If documenting children's learning is new to you and your colleagues, we offer some suggestions and some documentation prompts for you as you embrace inquiry learning and teaching. Some educators we have observed, collaborated with, or coached have successful systems for keeping track of children's progress, while others struggle with this important daily responsibility. If you are in this latter group, we hope you can find a system that works for you. Some of you may have already ordered steno pads, Post-it notes, and clipboards so you can form the habit of jotting down observations or the remarkable ideas that are provoked as children wonder, strategize, and resolve problems. Some of you may be using an app that assists with communicating with parents, including photos and notes. One recent discovery that some of us have embraced is a voice-to-text app for your phone so that you can document children's learning while you are elbows-deep in meal preparation, a diaper change, or a messy investigation with infants and toddlers. In Figures 3.8 through 3.11, we offer some examples of assessment tools that we have used or observed others using for documenting children's actions.

Copies of the assessment forms shown in Figures 3.8 and 3.9 could be placed on clipboards for each of the educators, with one sheet for each child to be observed. You should designate one educator to gather the sheets at the end of the week so

Figure 3.8. Weekly Observations

Child: _____________ Week of: _____________ P or V (photo/video)				
Monday	Tuesday	Wednesday	Thursday	Friday
Observations	Observations	Observations	Observations	Observations

Figure 3.9. Class Observations

Child: ____________	Date: ______ Time: ______	Activity: __________
What the Child Is Doing: **Photo or Video ______**	**What the Educator Is Saying or Doing:**	**What This Might Mean:**

Figure 3.10. Fieldnotes

Child: __________ Activity or Center: ________	Date:___________ Time: ____________
Observations	**Comments**

documentation can be added to the child's portfolio. You should make a note next to observations that have a photo or video to accompany them. You also may choose to identify the time of day, to determine optimal learning times for infants and toddlers.

LEARNING STORIES

There are several ways that learning stories can be used in infant and toddler classrooms. The following idea was gleaned from Carol Anne Wien's book *The Power of Emergent Curriculum: Stories from Early Childhood Classrooms* (2014). There are other resources describing how learning stories can be used to document learning and honor children and families, including early educators who have written extensively about learning stories (Carr & Lee, 2012, 2019; Drummond, 2017). Learning stories start with at least one photograph or preferably a series of photographs that help tell the story you are trying to communicate to children and families (see Figures 3.12 and 3.13). Learning stories communicate information about a child, not only to the child and their family but also to other educators, other children, classroom visitors, and the writers themselves. Learning stories can be copied and shared with families to facilitate discussions that can go deeper than typical checklists. They can be added to the classroom documentation space and placed in a child's portfolio to add to other information that has been gathered about the child.

Child: Landon Activity or Center: Chutes and Silos		Date: 4-8-18 Time: 9:15
Observations		**Comments**
Landon began to use the tubes as a container for the wooden and plastic block people. He started by filling the long, blue tube with people. When it was filled, he turned to the wide red tube and began picking up more block people to drop into the red tube. He picked up people with two hands and rotated or flipped them when they did not go into the tube on the first attempt. Several times he picked up more than one object in one hand. He looked carefully through the bin before selecting a block figure. He lifted the blue tube after filling it and watched as the people slid out of the bottom. He picked up the red tube and noticed that the people were not inside the tube. He set the blue tube down and dropped the people back into the red tube. He tipped the tube so that he could reach more people without laying the tube down. He filled the tubes for 6–8 minutes.		Landon was engaged for several minutes as he planned what materials he was going to use with the chutes and silos. He noticed that there was a problem with the block people and devised a strategy for getting more people in the tube. We will introduce some new balls next time. I want to see what he does with balls that fit and balls that do not fit in the tubes. How will he solve this problem?
Ryann was playing with Andrea and a small group of peers. Ryann saw what Landon was doing and went to the shorter red tube. She picked it up and all of the people fell out on the floor. Landon turned and saw what she had done and he moved to the tube to inspect the "damage." Andrea turned to talk to him and asked him what happened. He started to pick up some of them and then moved to the books. He picked a book and walked to an adult with the book in the air. He settled into a comfy chair with Paige and listened to several stories.		Landon is often a leader and innovator with STEM investigations. When he has a new idea other children observe and sometimes imitate his actions. Landon is patient with his friends and does not become upset when someone wants to use the materials he is using. He will just walk away from a potential conflict and find something else that engages him.

Child:	Date:	Experience:
Add photo		**What is happening?**
What might this mean?		
What have you seen at home?		
Plans for further learning:		

Child: Mariel	Date: 4-14-18	**Experience:** Unplanned opportunity with materials from open shelves

Mariel Opens a Jar

What is happening?

Mariel found a basket filled with small containers on the shelves near where an educator was reading to another child. She found a small jar and used her fine-motor skills to try to turn the lid and open it. She was unable to open it and communicated to the adult that she needed help. The adult showed her how to turn the lid to open it. Mariel used persistence to turn the lid as she held the jar in her other hand. She was able to open it after several attempts. When she had it opened she communicated to the adult to share her success. She continued to investigate the jar and the lid with her hands and fingers and then put it near her mouth and blew into it. She produced a sound with the jar and then turned to the lid and made a sound with the lid. She continued to investigate sounds with the jar and lid and communicated her discoveries to the educator several times.

What might this mean?

Mariel is communicating to her educator her need for help with the jar. After her educator demonstrates to Mariel how to twist the lid, Mariel used problem solving and persistence to do it all by herself. She made a sound with the jar and decided that it was interesting, so she produced more sounds by investigating the possibilities.

What have you seen at home?

Ask parents to share with you what Mariel is doing at home.

Plans for further learning:

We think that Mariel and her friends would be interested in investigating sound with other common household materials. We will introduce some new materials in the coming weeks.

Part II

STEM TOPICS TO USE WITH INFANTS AND TODDLERS

Introduction to Part II
Observing Infants and Toddlers During STEM Experiences

One question often asked by infant and toddler educators is how they should teach children in order to expand their STEM capabilities. In a busy day filled with caring routines, such as diaper changes, feeding, napping, and ensuring the safety of young children, it is overwhelming to try to "teach" STEM as well as to attend to the many other responsibilities in an infant or toddler classroom. Many educators feel unprepared to plan experiences that focus on STEM, and professional development opportunities often are centered on health and safety rather than on curriculum. Educators may be confused about the materials they need to purchase or prepare for STEM learning opportunities. We would suggest that STEM opportunities are in evidence throughout the infant and toddler classroom, in daily routines and in the materials that are already on the shelves.

Just as educators check classroom materials for safety, they must continue to do that with any new materials they add to encourage STEM explorations. Concern about choking is a primary issue for infants and toddlers who regularly mouth objects. Materials such as plastics should be checked daily for cracks or broken areas that may be sharp or cause pinching. Such objects should be removed from the children's access immediately. Sanitizing materials is a regular process, and should be continued with STEM materials. In addition to these considerations, Chapters 4–9 include specific ideas for safety and convenience that are related to those particular materials and experiences.

FINDING THE STEM IN CLASSROOM ROUTINES AND EXPERIENCES

In high-quality early learning environments, responsive educators take advantage of unplanned opportunities to discover what children might be wondering about and then provide materials and opportunities that encourage them to follow their interests. When children are included as co-developers of curriculum, there are endless opportunities for them to build confidence in their abilities and to form the trusting relationships that are at the center of the responsive classroom.

We think of cooperation with a hyphen added. Children and their educators co-operate in the classroom. That is, they develop a mutual trust that encourages everyone to share ideas about how the classroom will work. Co-operation is especially important in infant and toddler classrooms where the educator's role is to set the stage for learning so that children can begin to construct knowledge and make meaning of the world. We see educators co-operate when they listen to children's ideas by observing their actions and intentions, and by respecting their work as learners. Educators who are skilled observers and listeners use this documentation in the decision-making process.

STEM is all around us—in everyday classroom routines, on the playground, in our homes and the homes of the children we serve, and in our communities. We would suggest that you are already "doing STEM" every day with the infants and toddlers who are in your care. With careful observation, documentation, and planning, you can make the most of the opportunities that are available to you and the children in your program. We think about some of the routines and experiences that make up the daily schedules of infant and toddler classrooms and about the definition of STEM we shared in Chapter 1.

NOTICING AND RESPONDING TO STEM IN THE CLASSROOM

Start this journey of finding STEM by observing closely over time during daily routines. Take the time to document what you are observing with notes, photos, and video. Educators who have investigated the materials before introducing them to children will become accomplished at anticipating where STEM is already happening in the classroom. In an example with Josh and Melissa, described in Chapter 4, an educator noticed a child's wonder at the snack table and planned an experience that would capitalize on his unasked questions. Educators can think about some other daily routines that have the possibility for children's wondering and strategizing, such as getting dressed for the outdoors, taking a walk, washing hands and preparing for mealtime, getting ready for rest time, picking up toys before lunch, or song and story time. Educators can take advantage of these endless opportunities for capitalizing on children's amazing curiosity.

When you have collected some examples, sit down with your team and discuss what you are all noticing and how you can support children's competence by responding as a collaborator in their learning. How can you use parallel talk and self-talk to describe the child's actions and the actions you are taking as you participate in the learning experience? What are some ways to expand on what children are saying by repeating it and building on it? Develop a vocabulary list to use in a STEM investigation or share ideas about how and when to intervene with questions and comments. This is reflective practice. Changing our beliefs about what constitutes best practice may feel daunting, but support from colleagues can assist educators in this journey as they examine their pedagogy, or how they teach.

STEM in Toys and Manipulatives

Using these observations and the documentation of children's interests can guide educators in their selection of materials for the classroom that will provide children with opportunities to engage in STEM learning. Providing open-ended materials that have many possibilities for wondering, strategizing, and resolving problems provides young children with the chance to engage in inquiry and science learning at a conceptual level (National Science Teachers Association [NSTA], 2014). Our own experiences with teaching and mentoring educators suggest that it is easy to fall into the trap of purchasing commercial materials that have a pleasing appearance to adults but only one purpose for children.

When selecting materials for your classroom shelves, think about the interests the children in the classroom have been pursuing and what experiences will be at just the right level of complexity so that they are intrigued, yet not frustrated. Compare notes with your colleagues and ask a few questions: Will this toy or material be safe for all the children in the classroom? Is this toy or material durable enough to withstand daily cleaning? Will this toy or material be of interest to the infants and toddlers in the classroom? Is there more than one way to use this toy or these materials? Will children find unique ways of using them? Is there a way to display and store them so that all children are able to access them? Are there enough interesting things for children to do? Are there so many things on the shelves that children can't identify what they want to do? Is there a way that children can connect the toys and materials to experiences they have had at home or at school? What safe and readily available recycled materials or loose parts can be included in children's play? How can the program get the most bang for the buck when purchasing materials for infant and toddler programs?

In Chapters 4 through 9 we have identified classroom experiences that include open-ended materials that are obtained easily, are sometimes free, and can be used with children from 0–3. We feel certain that you are already offering some open-ended and engaging experiences to children. Our hope is that these ideas can enhance the work you are doing and provide ideas for low-cost materials that will inspire inquiry for all children. Furthermore, we hope that the experiences that invite inquiry for children will inspire educators like you to engage in reflective practice that will promote the important work we do with infants and toddlers.

STEM in Pretend Play

Early on, young children begin imitating adults and the interactions they have observed (see Figure PII.1). We see young toddlers trying on mom's shoes and shuffling into the kitchen to demonstrate, rock a baby, or pick up a spoon in a toy kitchen and pretend to stir the soup. The housekeeping corner is a great place to add plastic containers with lids that can be opened and closed, filled with objects, or carried from one part of the room to another. Measuring cups and spoons will intrigue children and provide opportunities to think about big and small, and more or less. Adding pretend food to the shelves invites thinking about categorization as children place the plates on one shelf and the pizza slices on another during clean-up. Dress-up clothes provide endless hours of fun and a chance to practice self-care routines in a safe and unhurried environment, as well as concepts of spatial understanding about what will fit their bodies. These experiences build curiosity, confidence, and self-regulation, all necessary for children to successfully engage in STEM learning. Pretend play can be a vehicle for all manner of exploration and discovery.

STEM in Art

One example of the availability of STEM experiences in infant and toddler classrooms is the art area. Open-ended art experiences are part of many early childhood programs. We might think of the work that children do when they are engaged in painting, working with clay, or using loose parts to create a mosaic as a sensory experience, but we can easily unpack the STEM learning that might be taking place as children engage in work at the art center, whether these activities are provided indoors or outside (see Figure PII.2).

Science includes exploring materials and making predictions based on observations. Children are engaging in science when they use their fingers and hands to manipulate clay on a play mat or use tools to paint on a table or at an easel. They can observe closely how materials respond to their actions and can predict what will happen when they pound, roll, and poke the clay, or when choosing a sponge rather than a paintbrush to spread paint on paper. Children

Figure PII.1. Exploring STEM in the Pretend Center

Figure PII.2. Outdoor Painting With Watermelon

are engaging in technology when they use the tools that are available in novel ways or when they identify a problem with their results if too much water is loaded on their paint brush and they try a new strategy with the paint and water. When painting outside with water, children can not only see how water affects surfaces to make them wet, but also how the water evaporates and leaves surfaces dry after the sun shines on them. Engineering is evident when a child moves tiles around on their work mat or decides to stack them rather than place them in a line while working with loose parts. We see evidence of developing mathematics skills when children experiment with different-sized paintbrushes and notice that the strokes vary in width, when they discover that they do not have enough clay to make a long snake, or when they use their developing spatial awareness to arrange materials so that they can be reached easily from their seat. When educators begin to find the STEM in everyday activities and routines, they have the opportunity to support young children as they engage in inquiry learning, not just in a few identified STEM experiences, but throughout each and every day.

Sensory Experiences

The earliest learning for infants happens through the senses, so providing frequent opportunities for young children to actively explore their world through sensory play is essential to brain development. Children have a wide range of responses to sensory input, so being a careful gatekeeper of the variety and intensity of sensory experiences is an important aspect of the educator's role. In addition, sensory experiences provide a multitude of opportunities for STEM learning. When children actively use their senses during play, connections are built in the brain. These early experiences promote the growth of cognition and the development of problem-solving skills, enhance language development, support motor development, and provide opportunities for social interactions with adults and peers. In our view, young children need daily opportunities to engage in sensory exploration. These experiences should be varied and available to children when they demonstrate interest. Young children need multiple and varied opportunities to engage in science exploration and discovery (NAEYC, 2014; NSTA, 2014).

Sensory play is a natural way for infants and young children to explore their environment with all of their senses. Many sensory activities for infant and toddler classrooms can be done with materials that are already available to you or are obtained easily and are inexpensive.

When educators plan sensory play for infants and young children, safety must come first. Plan the experience for a time when there will be constant supervision for the children who are engaged in the experience. With water, sand, beans, bubbles, or other sensory materials, there should be an adult who is in constant attendance at the tub or table. Selecting a time when some children are engaged in another activity, sleeping, or eating can ensure that there is an appropriate adult–child ratio. Seating children at a table with trays or small bins may be another way to introduce sensory materials safely, including a variety of tools or containers that accommodate children's ability to grasp and scoop the sensory materials. Children have individual needs and preferences when engaging in sensory play, so to ensure that those needs are being addressed, provide an invitation to play rather than an expectation that all children must engage with the same materials at the same time.

These examples of the pretend play center, the art center, toys and manipulatives, and the sensory center are just a few of the substantial opportunities for recognizing the STEM already in place in infant and toddler classrooms. We encourage educators to inventory their environments and to notice the many ways for young children to engage in STEM naturally throughout the day.

CHAPTER 4

Exploring Water With Infants and Toddlers: More Than Sensory

Jill Uhlenberg and Sherri Peterson

> ### TEXTBOX 4.1. COUNTING WATER DROPS
>
> Melissa served morning snack to the toddlers—graham crackers and sippy cups of water. She sat with the children and conversed with them about the morning's activities. She noticed that Josh had stopped eating and was watching water slowly drip from his upturned sippy cup. Each drop fell onto the tabletop or a cracker, and he watched patiently until the next drip formed and fell. Seeing Josh's interest, Melissa wrote a note to remind herself to place extra sippy cups in the water table during the morning exploration time the next day.
>
> Josh discovered a problem, and he wondered how the water was dripping out of the sippy cup spout rather than coming out more quickly. He observed carefully, waiting to see what happened in his investigation. Rather than using the typical strategies of very young children, such as shaking or banging the cup, he was patient as the water drops formed.

We might ask, "Where is the STEM in this unplanned activity?" Melissa noticed Josh's interest in the drips coming from his cup and wanted to capitalize on his interest. Careful observation is necessary to unpack what he might be thinking and wondering as he watches the drips. He may be wondering how long it will take to empty the cup, why the water is moving to the edge of the table, why his graham cracker is soggy rather than crisp, how he can get the water to drip faster, or why the drips are slower as the cup empties. With children in this age group, careful observation of their actions can give us insight into the hypotheses they are forming, their interests and curiosities, and what might promote their further exploration and investigation. In her book *Really Seeing Children*, Deb Curtis (2017) stated that as an early childhood educator, she has "developed the practice of waiting before jumping into a situation to determine what the thinking might be underneath a child's behavior" (p. 21). For some educators it may take practice and gentle reminders from a colleague, mentor, or instructional coach to observe quietly as young children struggle to solve a problem. This is inquiry learning and teaching.

Melissa observed Josh's interest in the dripping water and wanted to provide a planned opportunity based on her observations of his exploration so that he could continue to wonder, question, hypothesize, strategize, and come to a resolution that he found satisfying. Her decision to add a variety of sippy cups with lids to the water table was an intentional choice based on her careful observations. She wanted to provide a novel experience that was similar, yet different from previous investigations, so that Josh and his peers could activate prior knowledge and build on it.

Melissa's understanding about the role adults play in promoting, nurturing, and building on children's interests impacted the decisions she made when planning for the toddlers in her classroom. When educators reflect on their observations and documentation as they select materials and experiences, young children have opportunities to engage in learning that is meaningful to them and engages them over long periods of time.

Young children engage in STEM every day in both planned and unplanned experiences. In this instance, Josh made a discovery with his cup and engaged in careful examination of the way that water dripped from the tiny holes in the spout when the cup was tipped. Young children have a natural interest in learning more about the world around them, and engage in wondering and discovering during daily routines as well as during planned activities. They use their senses to develop conceptual understanding that forms the foundation for STEM learning. These discoveries can occur during classroom routines with everyday materials or in carefully orchestrated learning experiences that have been planned by educators and that are based on observation and documentation.

Melissa observed Josh's exploration and allowed him to continue. She might have urged him to stop making a mess or wasting his drink. Instead, she recognized his sudden interest in a new experience. Her decision to add sippy cups to the water table encouraged Josh and others to explore this everyday container in a new way (see Figure 4.1). Melissa used her observation to plan for a new set of experiences for the children.

Figure 4.1. Sippy Cups in the Water Table

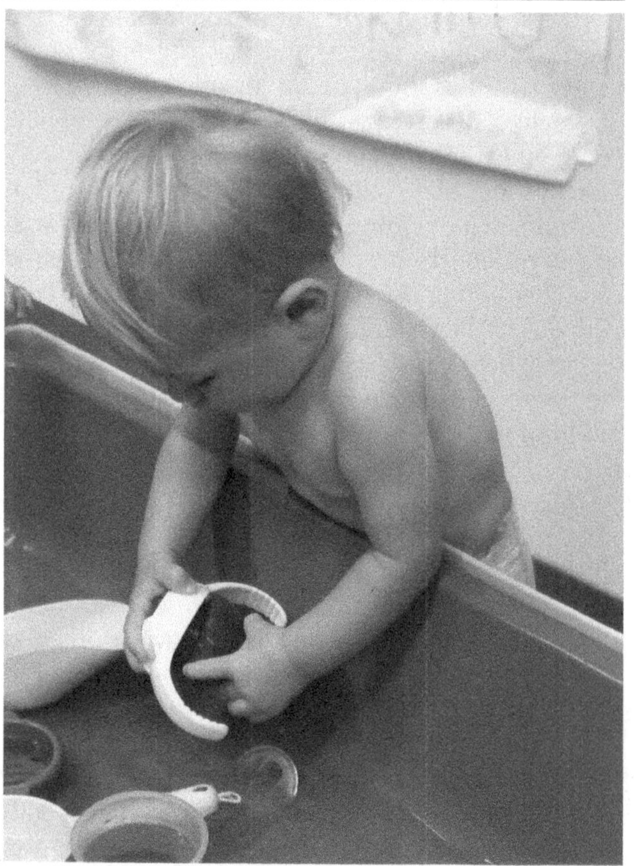

WHY WATER WITH INFANTS AND TODDLERS?

Water is a responsive material. That is, it responds to our actions on it in different ways than solid materials. For all ages, touching or immersing parts of our bodies in water provides sensory and emotional reactions. Even infants are soothed by water sights, sounds, or touch. Many adults think that infants or toddlers are too young to explore water, or that they can do it only in a messy way. Our experiences have been positive with very young children because we planned carefully and with the mess in mind.

Planning to keep children safe is a priority. Floors become slippery when wet, so towels or rugs thrown down around the water container will support mobile children's abilities to stand or move around. These may need to be changed as the towels or rugs become soaked, so adults must be prepared. We also found that indoor entry mats with rubber backing worked well to keep floors safe. If temperatures are warm enough, either inside or outside, infants and toddlers may strip down to diapers during water exploration. If possible, working outdoors avoids much of the mess.

Keeping water levels low and children under constant supervision are also necessary to prevent children from leaning or falling into the water containers. At least one adult, depending on the number of children, should remain at the water container while the materials are in use.

Adults should be alert to children attempting to drink the water. This is especially true for the youngest children because they tend to mouth all materials. If children are well hydrated, they may explore the materials instead of drinking. Adults may need to offer water exploration following snack time.

Toddlers who have had many opportunities to explore water will focus on their explorations. We even found that handwashing at the sink became less messy when toddlers had experienced water regularly in the classroom. Once the children had the basic understanding of water and its characteristics, they were more able and interested in exploring how water interacts with other materials and the environment (see Figure 4.2).

In the next sections we describe how children demonstrated the ITILM and educators employed the ITM. Using examples from our observations, we show how the models can be used with water

Figure 4.2. Exploring Water and Sponges

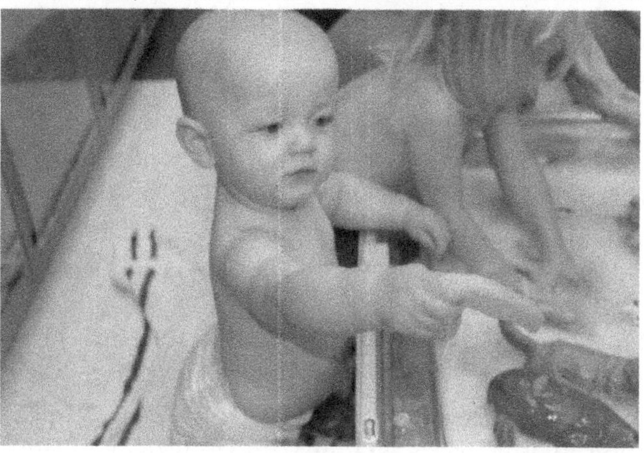

experiences in general, and then we address each developmental level of infants and toddlers (infants, young toddlers, and older toddlers). A key component to both models is observation. With careful observation, an educator can use the ITILM to understand the child's inquiry and then can use the ITM to make decisions on ways to support that inquiry.

TEXTBOX 4.2. DAVID SHARES IDEAS ABOUT WATER

David stood at the side of a small plastic dishpan on the floor. The dishpan held 2 inches of water as well as three small new sponges, cut into 3-inch square pieces, and a few other plastic objects. At 11 months, David could pull up to stand but was not yet walking independently. Earlier he had noticed that the sponges held water until he squeezed them. Then the water drizzled down his arm and back into the tub. He watched this happen repeatedly, dropping the sponge into the water and then squeezing to empty it. Each time he looked at Emily, the infant room educator who was seated on the floor opposite David. Emily responded to David each time by narrating his actions: "You put the sponge in the water. You squeezed the sponge. The water came out."

David stopped his actions for a moment and looked at the wall behind Emily. In this classroom, educators had placed laminated rebus signs at low levels around the room so that the children could see family photos of the different infants in the room, as well as common objects that the infants saw or used daily. The sign behind Emily showed a faucet with water coming out with the word *water* printed below it.

David crawled to the wall, still holding the dripping sponge, and held the sponge up to the sign depicting a faucet with water coming out. He pushed the sponge against the faucet sign, squeezing it so that the water dribbled out. He looked at Emily with a smile and waited for her response.

WATER EXPLORATION WITH INFANTS

Young infants who are not yet mobile will need support from educators in their exploration of water. These activities also will be limited in their scope until the children are more mobile. Infants will have experienced water in basic ways, such as washing their hands and face with a cloth, and have been in the sink or tub at bath time. They also may have seen objects containing water or other liquids. The educators will be providing very basic interactions at this point.

Infant Toddler Inquiry Learning Model With Water Exploration

Young children find water fascinating. Their natural curiosity leads to many ideas about how water affects objects, lifting some to the water's surface while others sink to the bottom of the water container. Although infants and toddlers, and even many adults, do not understand why this happens, there is no need to try to explain the reasons why. The value is in the wondering and investigating of materials and trying out objects to see what happens.

David investigated materials, and he repeated his actions as he wet the sponges and then squeezed them. He even demonstrated for Emily how the sponge first held water and then released it when he squeezed.

David may have been thinking about water in other parts of the room as he looked at the sign showing a faucet. Emily's commentary on his actions also included the word *water* so that David may have connected that word with his actions. He appeared to create that connection by taking the sponge to the sign and demonstrating to Emily that he understood the source of the water. While this did not appear as a specific problem to be solved by David, his actions did indicate that he was making connections in his mind and had resolved his own question about where the water came from. Another child may have explored in a very different way.

Inquiry Teaching Model With Water Exploration

Emily capitalized on even these youngest children's natural curiosity about water. She knew that they had limited prior experiences with water and stimulated interest by providing the water experience and sponges. She observed David's actions and supported communication by narrating his activity. When David took the sponge and moved toward the sign on the wall, she could have stopped him to avoid the water dripping, but instead she facilitated his exploration by allowing him to take the wet sponge away from the water tub. Emily also fostered communication when David placed the sponge on the faucet sign as she remarked that he was correct—that the faucet was where the water came from.

Emily made the decision to allow David to take the wet sponge away from the water tub because she knew he had something in mind. She was able to document this event as confirmation that David had a clear understanding of the source of water in the room.

Water With Infants

Water is commonly found in most classrooms for young children. Educators may not have allowed infants to explore water, except as a sensory experience. We contend that sensory experiences still support STEM learning as children construct physical knowledge of water's characteristics. Adding other materials to the water then supports children's construction of logical-mathematical knowledge as they explore relationships between the water and the added materials. Understanding water is a long-term and complex process, with many adults still unsure of how some items sink or float, processes of evaporation or surface tension, and more. Introducing water allows infants to begin developing basic ideas that will expand as they grow older and experience more interactions with water.

ITM: *Engaging Infants.* Infants are interested in and curious about their world. Water is a natural part of their day, whether adults or children are washing hands or drinking, and is a common material. That makes water interesting to the infants on multiple levels. Little encouragement is needed from educators to capitalize on this as an engaging material for children.

ITM: *Providing Opportunities.* Educators can begin with simple activities that will spark curiosity for infants. Infants may be seated in an infant seat or held upright on an educator's lap. Some educators may begin with sealed containers that allow the water within to move, giving infants an opportunity to observe visually how the water acts. Other opportunities may include more than just visual appeal, so that infants may experience touch, taste, and smell through their senses.

For example, the educator may allow a wet cloth or eyedropper full of water, held above the infant's hands or arms, to drip water slowly. In this case, the infant may observe the water drops as well as feeling them hit the skin of their hands or arms. The educator may hand a wet washcloth to the child after cleansing hands and face following a meal or snack. Infants typically will suck on the wet cloth, or they may use the cloth to wipe a nearby surface.

Infants also may enjoy dipping arms or legs in a shallow container of water. This allows them to experience deeper exploration of touching the water, as well as observing how the water reacts to various movements. Educators may hold infants during this process, or if the children are able to sit upright unaided, the adults simply may remain close by, providing support as needed or commenting on the children's actions.

For infants who sit upright without support, a small amount of water on a cafeteria tray or a high-chair tray will provide opportunities for exploring water in many ways. Educators may expect the children to splash as they slap the water with their hands, bringing surprised looks from the children as the water responds to their movements. These infants also will enjoy sitting on the floor with small tubs or other flat containers of water and different objects. Pieces of paper will provide opportunities to explore textures of wet versus dry materials. Natural materials are also interesting objects to explore when wet and dry, including pine cones, seashells, or small pieces of wood with bark removed.

ITM: *Making Decisions.* Educators will discover many actions to document as the infants explore water. Children will experience cause and effect as they splash, or when paper is dropped into the water and absorbs the liquid, changing the texture of the paper. Observations also will provide educators with an understanding of what the children are thinking and understanding.

Educators may decide to foster communication by describing their own or the children's actions, or they may decide to simply observe as the infants engage with the water and other materials. These observations also will let educators know when children have tired of the experience, or when they would benefit by the addition of different materials, as well as when the children have been able to demonstrate developing physical abilities.

These observations also are important in understanding when a child's development may be lagging that of others. Documenting these observations is crucial to understanding when children need additional support from teachers or specialists, and in discussing a child's needs with parents and other family members.

Water With Young Toddlers

Just as infants easily are drawn to water explorations, young toddlers do not need encouragement to explore water. In fact, young children who are tentative about touching some materials, like fingerpaint, willingly engage in water experiences. The interest level remains high for long periods of time. We have found that some programs offer water experiences every day, changing out accessories from time to time, without toddlers becoming bored.

ITM: Engaging Young Toddlers. Young toddlers engage easily with water explorations. Because they experience water in a variety of ways throughout their day, they have a basic understanding of some of the uses of water, and the interest is there. Introducing new uses for water expands this level of interest.

Textbox 4.3. Ahsan Transfers Water

Ahsan was playing at the water center with his friends and his educator Sydney. He picked up a large plastic beaker in his left hand and a bulb syringe in his right hand. He filled the beaker and tipped it over to dump out the water (see Figure 4.3). Then he dropped the bulb syringe and used a plastic jar to fill the beaker. When the beaker was full, he picked up the bulb syringe and stuck it inside the beaker so that only the bulb was visible. He looked at Sydney, who said, "How can you get it out," then, "Oops," as he pulled it out. He looked inside the beaker and said, "Water," then picked it up and slid it through the water to fill it. He turned the syringe upside down and looked it over carefully, then started to place it into the beaker again. He stopped, turned it again, and inspected it. He dropped the beaker, then picked it up and attempted to squeeze water from the syringe into the beaker. He slowly pushed it into the beaker until it was inserted up to the bulb. He said, "Up," and jumped up while pulling the syringe out of the beaker. He looked at Sydney as he pulled it out and pointed the tube of the syringe in her direction. She said, "Oh, you want me to help you?" She placed her hand on top of his while holding the bulb of the syringe. She guided the baster to the water and said, "Squeeze," while she assisted him. Then she guided it to the beaker and squeezed until the baster was empty. She then allowed Ahsan to try it on his own. He pulled the baster out and shook it in her direction and said, "Help." Sydney guided the baster back to the water with one hand as she assisted another child who approached her. She assisted Ahsan once again to fill the syringe. Ahsan then put the beaker and baster back into the water and began to swish them both around in the water.

Here we can see how Sydney engaged Ahsan in a water investigation by adding some unfamiliar materials that captivated his interest as he explored their physical characteristics. She watched carefully as he attempted to fill the beaker and noticed his curiosity about the bulb syringe, and later with the funnel, but did not intervene until he tried it on his own and then looked to her for support. She approached him with respect for his efforts and paused to ask whether he wanted help. She guided him to fill and empty the syringe with her help before coaching him to do it on his own. Sydney's relationship with Ahsan and her knowledge about the way that he approached challenges guided her in decision-making about the timing of her support.

Figure 4.3. Ahsan Explores a Syringe and Beaker

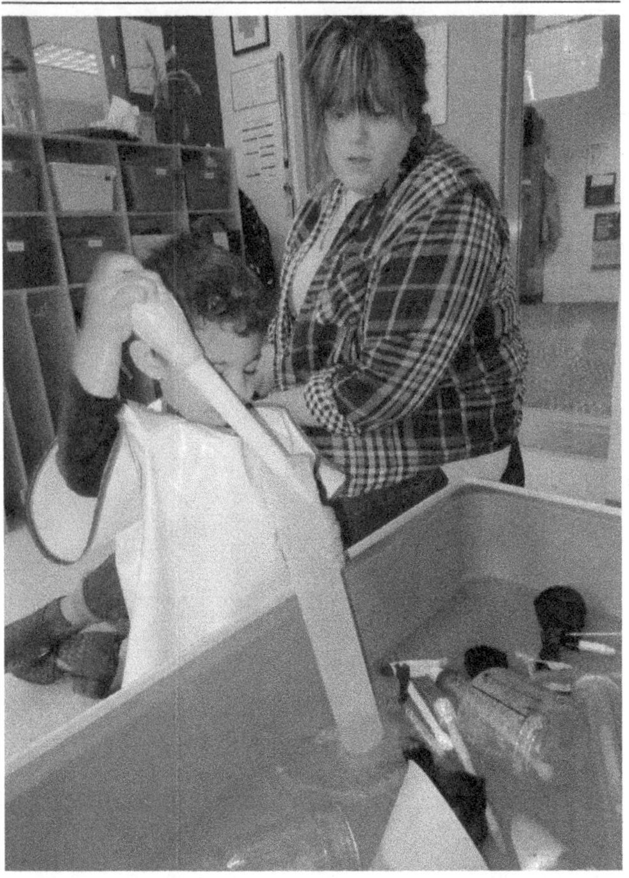

ITM: Providing Opportunities. Offering explorations that are messy by adult standards takes preparation. Educators who are comfortable with messy situations will encourage children's experiences with less concern about how to keep areas clean and neat. In addition, some classrooms provide plastic aprons for children's messy experiences, and adults may need to secure dry clothing for children who engage with water play.

Preparing for water exploration may require good communication and planning between adults in the environment so that the focus for the children is on learning and exploring. This can be challenging for some educators whose focus is on keeping the environment in order. Educators who know what to expect from the toddlers in their care, because they have observed and documented the children's dispositions and development, will be better prepared for the unexpected events that occur in all classrooms.

Sydney and her teaching partner had introduced water experiences early in the school year when these young toddlers moved from the infant classroom. They knew that the educators in the infant classroom had provided opportunities for the children to investigate water during their first year. They observed and documented the children's interests as they played, then provided additional materials as children's motor skills developed and their focus shifted.

Before they introduced the bulb syringes, the educators had observed the interest the children had in activating the small squeeze bottles that were part of the water exploration. The toddlers had been scooping water to fill the bottles and then matching the lids to the bottles before asking for assistance to secure them so they could squirt water into the tub (and onto one another). Sydney and her teaching partner made a decision to add the bulb syringes as a new challenge for the toddlers. They provided bulbs for the water center and also included larger squeeze bottles so there would be challenges at everyone's skill level. They continued to monitor children's interests and added new tools and materials as children indicated they were ready for novel materials.

ITM: Making Decisions. Sydney was aware that Ahsan frequently came to STEM centers to use the materials. He was interested in figuring things out independently and did not approach adults for assistance when he was unsuccessful. Often, he would use one strategy and then leave the center or become upset when this strategy did not produce the results he expected. When adults attempted to facilitate his exploration, he would turn away from them. During this encounter, Sydney waited for his appeal for help to activate the syringe, observed and documented his efforts, and then provided hand-over-hand assistance when he indicated that he needed assistance to accomplish his goal. She waited for Ahsan to try squeezing the bulb after her instruction and then assisted him again when he indicated that he wanted her help to try again. She continued to give Ahsan opportunities to try out the new strategy she had modeled for him, and documented his efforts by videotaping and taking photographs so that she could discuss Ahsan's approach to this problem with her teaching partner during their planning time.

During prior investigations, Sydney had documented Ahsan's response to frustration and was thrilled to document his perseverance during this water activity. In those previous observations, Ahsan had tried new experiences for very short periods of time before becoming frustrated. During several activities he had cried or screamed when his attempts to solve a problem or use a new strategy did not produce the results he expected. He typically did not ask for assistance when his efforts were unsuccessful. Ahsan's persistence with the syringe was a new approach to learning for him and one that Sydney and her teaching partner had set as a goal for him.

At their next planning meeting they discussed other STEM experiences and specific materials that might engage Ahsan so that he could continue to persevere with difficult tasks and would ask an adult or a peer for assistance when he was unsuccessful. They anticipated that Ahsan's family would be delighted that he had approached this problem with such intention.

> ### Textbox 4.4. Filling Funnels
>
> On another day, Ahsan and several other toddlers explored the water table where a new set of funnels had been added. Ahsan held a funnel by the neck and poured water into the top of the funnel so that it ran out the bottom smoothly (see Figure 4.4). Ahsan's attention was on the water level above, and he did not notice the water running out the bottom of the funnel and down his arm back into the table, with some water hitting the floor. The two adults had covered the floor with towels, but around Ahsan, these towels quickly became soaked. Anna, an educator, spoke with Ahsan and pointed out the water that ran down Ahsan's arm. Ahsan did not respond to her words and just kept pouring water into the funnel.

Anna's intervention may have been designed to promote deeper thinking, or she simply may have intended to encourage Ahsan to keep the water in the water table as he worked. However, he was interested only in pouring water into the funnel, so she decided to support his investigation rather than insist on keeping dry at the risk of frustrating Ahsan. She fostered communication by describing Ahsan's actions and the water's movements as he worked. When Ahsan did not respond to her comments, she recognized that this is a common reaction for young toddlers. Because Anna knew this, she did not expect Ahsan to answer

Figure 4.4. Ahsan Fills a Funnel

her or to change his actions at the time. Instead, she noted his attention and actions on a notepad, with the intention of documenting his learning and tracking his water exploration with the funnels.

Water With Older Toddlers

Older toddlers typically have had many experiences with water, in routine activities as well as sensory table use. They will be excited to engage with interesting tools and containers and will continue exploring their fascination with water.

ITM: Engaging Older Toddlers. Older toddlers will delight you with their enthusiasm for the water center, whether indoors or out (see Figure 4.5). Their

Figure 4.5. Rosalyn and Jonathon Investigate Water

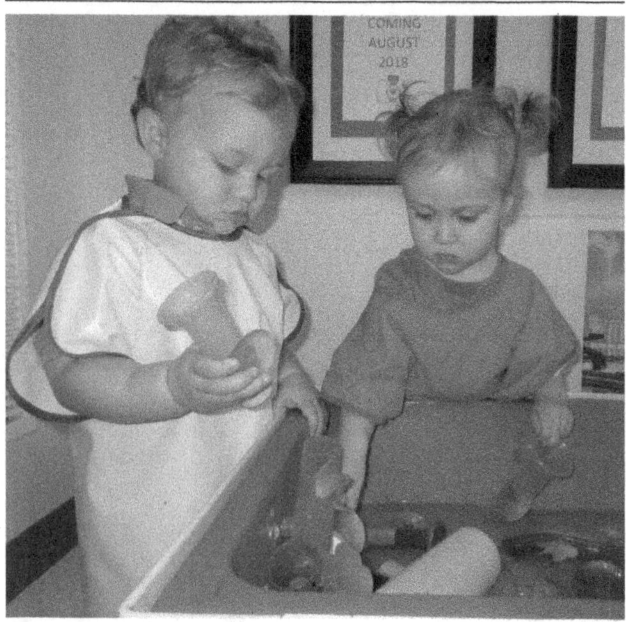

prior experiences with water may include bathtubs, wading pools, or even trips to the beach. Before planning water investigations, use your newsletter or social media to encourage families to share the experiences children have participated in outside of school. Knowledge about what children know or already can do will assist you in planning for new learning. It also may be a great time to collaborate with the other infant and toddler educators to determine what kinds of water activities have been included in the curriculum for those children who have been with your program since infancy.

Textbox 4.5. Rosalyn Fills a Beaker

Rosalyn saw the educator, Maria, sitting near the water table in a corner of the classroom. She joined Maria and stuck her hands into the water. She picked up a large, translucent beaker and tipped the water out. She dropped it and splashed the water with one hand. She looked at Maria to see whether her educator was observing her actions.

She began to splash again as Maria handed her a tiny scoop. Rosalyn grabbed it and said "Oh, yeah." She attempted to get water from a large container, but had it positioned upside-down. Maria said, "Did you get any?" Rosalyn smiled as Maria replied, "Not quite."

Rosalyn picked up a large measuring cup, dumped out the water, and dropped it into the water table, then picked up a beaker filled with water and dumped it. Maria said, "That was a LOT of water." Rosalyn continued to pick up containers to dump water from them.

When she splashed a bit, Maria commented, "Whoa," and Rosalyn repeated her comment. Rosalyn stopped her investigation momentarily. Maria then picked up a small beaker and asked, "Can you put water in here?" Rosalyn looked as Maria filled the small beaker with water from a larger container and said, "Here, watch." Rosalyn grabbed the beaker to dump the water. Maria said, "You just don't want water in any of these, do you?"

Rosalyn filled a beaker while Maria observed and said, "You just wanted to do it yourself." Maria picked up another container. "How about this one?" Rosalyn giggled. Maria held the measuring cup with one hand as Rosalyn continued to fill containers and dump them.

She picked up an inverted cup and tipped it as if to dump it. Maria noticed by saying, "Oh, what happened to the water?" Rosalyn said something unintelligible and picked up a small beaker to fill it. She positioned it inside the large measuring cup that Maria was holding. She attempted to tip it into the measuring cup but was unsuccessful, as it was too large to tip while inside the measuring cup. Maria remarked, "Oh, that's interesting." Rosalyn dumped the water into the table while Maria picked up a larger beaker and the measuring cup. She said, "Wait, can you fill this one now?" and indicated the beaker. Rosalyn said, "Yeah, that's fun." Maria picked up both of them, indicating that Rosalyn should fill the measuring cup instead of the beaker. "Can you put it back in this one?" she asked, while demonstrating. "Can you find a smaller one?" she asked, while pointing to the measuring cup. Rosalyn continued to fill containers and dump the water into the water table while Maria observed and documented Rosalyn's work.

In this classroom, Maria knew, Rosalyn had participated in water experiences many times as a young toddler, so she wanted to include some new materials in the water center. She found a variety of large and small scoops with the recycled materials and added these as well as some plastic beakers of different sizes. When Rosalyn came to the center, she chose a tiny scoop and a large beaker. Maria waited to see what strategies Rosalyn would use with these new materials and what her goal might be as she began her investigation.

ITM: Providing Opportunities. Maria invited Rosalyn's investigations by sitting near her at the water table and providing support to her as she tried out several strategies with the new materials. She observed for several minutes as she documented Rosalyn's movements by taking photos and video. She fostered Rosalyn's language and vocabulary development by describing what Rosalyn was doing, using mathematical vocabulary, and repeating and expanding on Rosalyn's expressive language. She facilitated Rosalyn's exploration by demonstrating techniques and noticing her work but did not interfere with the ideas that Rosalyn had about filling and dumping the water. Her relationship with Rosalyn as a learner was evident when she let Rosalyn take the lead on the investigation, displaying confidence in her problem-solving abilities and her decisions about how to fill the containers.

ITM: Making Decisions. Maria made instructional decisions throughout her interaction with Rosalyn. She knew that by supporting Rosalyn's investigation she would have the opportunity to document her learning in several curricular areas, including approaches to learning, language and literacy, math, science, and social–emotional development. Educators who include STEM investigations in their plans for children tend to use highly effective teaching practices, including asking attention-focusing questions, encouraging children to observe carefully and predict results, introducing relevant vocabulary, and helping to scaffold children's thinking and planning (Greenfield et al., 2017). Maria used wait time effectively as she observed Rosalyn's actions in order to check for understanding and promote deeper thinking. Her relationship with Rosalyn and her knowledge about the way that Rosalyn approached problems enabled her to give just the right amount of support.

EDUCATOR PLANNING FOR WATER INVESTIGATIONS

Throughout each day, infants and toddlers are engaging in STEM experiences when educators provide open-ended materials that are selected to draw children in and to stimulate their senses. In her book *Infants and Toddlers at Work* (2010), Ann Lewin-Benham describes the way that educators in Reggio Emilia schools select materials for infants and toddlers: "Reggio teachers consider each material's individuality and unusual features such as shape, pressure, temperature, and the movements children must make to use the material" (p. 62). By selecting materials that have many interesting properties, educators are inviting curiosity, problem solving, and encouraging exploration and investigation, concept development, and engagement in all of the STEM disciplines.

Selecting Materials

If you are ready for some new challenges in the water center, the selection of materials will be an essential factor in moving from sensory play to a STEM investigation. When selecting materials for the water center, safety is first and foremost. Plastic materials should be durable and free from sharp edges or cracks. Other features to consider:

- Is the material durable?
- Is it appropriate for the developmental levels of the children?
- Can all children access the materials and participate in the experience?
- Does it involve the child in play?
- Is there something to figure out?
- Does it work as intended?
- Is there more than one way to use it?
- Have you selected the right amount of materials so that everyone can be engaged, but you can monitor children's investigations?
- Does it fit into your budget?
- Does it require preparation?
- Do you have a place for materials to dry before storing?

Materials for Water Investigations in Infant Classrooms

- Plastic tubs or dishpans, or a small water table made for infants who are sitting and standing (see Figure 4.3)
- Cafeteria trays, cake pans (see Figure 4.6)

Figure 4.6. Water in a Cake Pan

- Towels or rugs
- Translucent and transparent beakers, graduated cylinders, measuring cups, and pitchers
- Translucent and transparent plastic containers with lids of varying sizes, including sippy cups
- Plastic balls of varying sizes and composition, including water balls and Nerf Balls that will absorb water
- Ping-pong balls, small whiffle balls, and golf balls
- Funnels
- Sponges of varying sizes
- Sieves or strainers
- Soup ladles and slotted spoons
- Plastic cheese, salt, or sugar shakers

Materials for Water Investigations in Toddler Classrooms (in Addition to Infant Materials)

- Water table designed for toddlers or one that has adjustable legs
- Vinyl smocks
- Translucent and transparent squeeze bottles and containers, such as shampoo, ketchup, lotion, dish soap, or bath products, with lids of differing sizes and with differing hole sizes
- Spray bottles (see Figure 4.7)
- Eyedroppers or pipettes

Figure 4.7. Enya Fills a Spray Bottle With Water

- Bottle brushes
- Bulb basters
- Natural materials such as wood scraps, pine cones, shells, rocks, leaves, or twigs
- Corks
- Clear plastic cups with holes drilled in bottom and sides—a variety of sizes and configurations
- Plastic water pump that is easy to activate

Water provides endless opportunities for young children to explore and problem-solve, as well as to engage in a relaxing sensory experience. In Chapter 9 you will read about water as a source of sound exploration as well. We have seen classrooms where water is a daily choice for toddlers, with always at least one child who chooses the water table during center time. Educators can provide a wide variety of materials to engage children's interest and extend their actions as they lay a foundation for later learning about water.

CHAPTER 5

Contents and Containers

Spatial Understanding and Mathematics

Jill Uhlenberg and Rosemary Geiken

TEXTBOX 5.1. HADLEY FILLS A COLANDER

Eleven-month-old Hadley placed a ball inside a colander with a handle (see Figure 5.1). She bounced the colander up and down and watched the ball move. When she took it out of the colander she said, "ball." She squeezed the ball and then replaced it in the colander. She looked at the adult to see whether she was watching. When the ball flipped out of the colander, she replaced it with another toy. She observed the results and then grabbed the ball again and bounced it inside the colander. She dropped the ball, retained the colander, and then crawled to an educator. She batted the colander from side to side and put it on her head. She said "ball" several times. The educator repeated the word and handed her the ball. The educator responded to her verbalizations with language and facial expressions. The educator handed Hadley the colander, and Hadley moved it up and down after the educator placed a larger ball inside. When the ball flipped out of the colander, the educator retrieved it. Hadley bounced it in the colander and then looked at the educator. At one point the ball flipped out and Hadley continued to move the colander up and down. Then she looked around on the floor, found the ball, and placed it in the colander after examining it carefully. She moved it up and down and then looked at another educator who was seated on the other side of her.

WHY CONTENTS AND CONTAINERS?

Educators who observe very young children will notice their desire to move things around, filling and emptying containers over and over, carrying collections of objects around the room, and mixing objects together in seemingly unplanned ways. One colleague called this the "pull and dump" phase, with children pulling items from shelves and dumping them on the floor or into various containers. We became curious about whether much learning was happening in this pull and dump phase, so we decided to analyze the children's actions to refine our understanding of the learning that can occur with very simple and inexpensive materials.

We observed children 12–36 months old in several settings as they explored a variety of plastic containers, some with lids and some that nested like canisters or measuring cups, as well as metal muffin tins. In addition to these containers, we also provided possible contents that might be of interest to these very young children. These objects included scarves, small blocks, and a variety of sizes of plastic ball pit–type balls and fabric splat balls. These materials were stored in two large tubs. Educators allowed children to add objects from within their classrooms to the tubs we provided (Uhlenberg & Geiken, 2020).

When we observed the children and analyzed their actions, we noticed that most of the children were exploring mathematical concepts, especially concepts that demonstrated developing spatial understanding. Spatial understanding is a component of mathematical thinking. When educators think about mathematics for this age group, many think first of counting and recognizing numerals. However, our experience has been that infants are beginning to explore space, and how objects fit in

Figure 5.1. Hadley Explores a Colander

space, before their first birthdays, well before they begin to think of counting and numerals.

Spatial Understanding

The development of basic spatial understanding is a slow process. Piaget and Inhelder (1967) wrote about infants and their perceptions of objects in space, such as whether an object is near or far away, or whether it is separate from other objects. Multiple perceptions about space develop at the same time, and in fact the perceptions support and build upon one another. These spatial understandings continue throughout childhood, emphasizing the importance of adults providing ongoing spatial experiences such as blocks, construction toys, and materials that encourage children to be creative. Later school experiences continue to develop spatial understanding and support the development of future athletes, dancers, architects, builders, artists, pilots, and others who rely on understanding space in their professions.

As educators observe very young children's developing understanding of space and how objects fill it, they can plan to introduce containers and possible contents that encourage exploration. Educators who have taken the time to explore contents and containers themselves, before introducing materials to the children, can gain this understanding more easily if they try to think about what the children will do. What will they try with materials? Knowing the infants and toddlers well will support the educators' abilities to plan and understand children's explorations, as well as to note surprises as children engage in ways that we don't expect. For example, Austin, 24 months old, wanted to play on his toy tractor. He held the adult's hand for support as he stood on one foot and lifted his other foot high in the air. He mounted the toy tractor, which was actually approximately 12 inches in length and 8 inches in height. Austin's spatial understanding of the comparative sizes of his body and his toy tractor were not yet complete. His actions were quite surprising to the educator watching this event.

Concrete Materials vs. Digital Screens

We strongly encourage educators to provide concrete materials to infants and toddlers rather than using digital screens. While there are digital applications available for very young children, these are concerning for several reasons. Kuhl (2010b) measured the brain engagement of infants who interacted both with real persons and with video screens. Although her focus was on language development, her results relate to spatial understanding as well. The babies in her study showed little to no brain activity when watching a two-dimensional screen showing an adult speaking. Interacting with a real person resulted in a vivid brain scan, with infants responding actively to the person speaking. That face-to-face time made all the difference.

Screen time is a strong trend in child-care and home settings. Very young children seem drawn to screens, as are adults. However, large amounts of screen time can undermine children's development of the basic perceptions of spatial understanding. In order to value exploration of real objects, we need to think about what infants and toddlers cannot learn from screens:

1. Sensory development—How things (including people) taste, smell, and feel. While screens can provide sound and colors, they limit the full sensory experiences involved with real objects.
2. Textures—These can be depicted visually, but screens cannot engage children with differences in textures other than visually. A screen showing a bumpy orange does not feel bumpy.
3. Depth perception—Very young infants begin their understanding of space with the concepts of near and far. Newborns have limited visual perception. As that develops, they are more able to view and understand what is nearby and what is further away (Piaget & Inhelder, 1967). On a screen, everything is the same distance from the infant—distant objects are smaller and nearby objects are larger, but to infants this may just appear to be size difference rather than "nearbyness."
4. Separation of objects—On a screen, every-thing is part of one thing—the screen. Real objects are separate from one another. Infants learn that objects are separate by grasping and handling them, turning them around, and noticing that the object has sides and a back.
5. Object permanence—This begins to develop early in life through learning the continuity of objects. By turning objects in their hands, babies learn that the object continues on different sides. Eventually, they understand that the objects remain solid even when out of sight.
6. Object constancy—A solid object's size and shape do not change. On a screen, we easily can enlarge or reduce objects. That real orange stays the same size and shape unless we do something to change it. Object constancy is the beginning of ideas about

conservation, an important concept in mathematical thinking, including spatial understanding. Piaget (1954) noted that young children were not able to conserve quantities or sizes until they were around 6 years old. This means that they did not understand that rearranging materials did not change their number, size, or volume. For example, at snack time two children each get three crackers. The first child's crackers are close together on the plate and are touching one another. The second child's crackers are spread out on the plate so they are not touching. The first child complains that the other child has more crackers! The first child has not learned to conserve quantity so doesn't understand that just because the other child's crackers appear to take up more room, the other child does not have more crackers.

Researchers Francis and Whitely (2015) report research on children's transfer of understandings about three-dimensional (3D) objects from work-ing with only two-dimensional (2D) objects, such as on a screen. They expressed concern that children between 6 months and 3 years of age make little transfer of spatial understanding between 2D and 3D objects. That is, understanding the characteris-tics of a circular shape on a screen does not support understanding what a spherical ball is like. They call this the *video deficit* effect and suggest that young children need experiences with 3D objects to really understand them.

Spatial Understanding and Mathematics

When provided with 3D materials, children in our observations consistently demonstrated mathemati-cal concepts of spatial understanding. The concepts we observed, and how we defined them, included the following:

- Accumulation—gathering a random variety of objects in a container with no planned organization; this is an early exploration of the space inside a container.
- Distribution—gathering a collection of objects repeatedly; using the same action on

the same or similar objects; an early type of organization or patterning.

- Collection—placing objects together that seem (to the toddlers) to belong together; an early form of classifying or categorizing.
- Nesting—placing an object inside a container and at least a third item inside the inner object or container; a more refined approach to collection as toddlers layer objects and containers.
- One-to-one correspondence—matching one object to one container; randomly at first, but with improving relationships as toddlers begin to better understand size and space. One-to-one correspondence is foundational to understanding counting and numbers.
- Creative construction—stacking containers and objects to build towers; this requires balance as unusually shaped objects and containers are placed on the tower.

As children play, they develop these concepts and are building a strong foundation for more complex spatial concepts they will encounter later in school. The study of children exploring Contents and Containers (C&C) began as we wondered what the children were learning when they were pulling and dumping materials, and continued as we observed how they explored simple plastic and metal containers and objects to put inside them. Our journey has led us to the realization of the importance of these explorations as the mathematical foundations of spatial understanding.

Infant Toddler Inquiry Learning Model With Contents and Containers

While we don't know what happened before Collette approached Mena, we can see that she clearly had identified a problem to solve—which lid to use on the ball in the bowl. She had wondered about which lid would work best, perhaps trying other lids before she brought her objects to Mena. As Collette tried first one lid and then the other, she explored the physical characteristics of the two lids she had brought to Mena.

As Collette strategized, observing how the materials worked or didn't work to solve her problem,

Figure 5.2. Collette Practices With Lids and Containers

her first solution (lid) did not appear to satisfy her criteria for the right lid, but the second solution (lid) did. Her acceptance of this approximate solution demonstrated her satisfaction, so far, with the strategies she was using.

Collette shared the materials and her work with Mena, an indication that she had resolved her problem, when she simply could have tried the two lids without Mena's assistance somewhere else in the room. At 17 months, Collette chose not to verbalize her questions or actions, which is not unusual for very young children. She observed how the first lid did not fit to her satisfaction. She repeated her actions with the second lid. Most interesting, Collette seemed to evaluate her actions and their results differently than adults might have done.

We would document this level of thinking and problem solving with the speculation that Collette was in the early processes of her spatial understanding. She demonstrated a developing sense of one-to-one correspondence, using one lid at a time for the container, showing she understood that a container has only one lid (see Figure 5.2). Mena would expect her to develop more and more accurate perceptions as she gained more experience through exploring the materials further.

Inquiry Teaching Model With Contents and Containers

Several actions of the ITM occurred in Mena's interactions with Collette. To engage the learners, Mena provided C&C materials that clearly stimulated interest and curiosity in examining objects to see how they interact. Through observation over time, she would note whether the toddlers lost interest, and she potentially would add to or change some of the materials available to reignite that curiosity. Or she might choose to move to another topic altogether, based on the children's interests.

Mena observed Collette and recognized the problem that she was attempting to solve. Mena supported problem solving, not by telling Collette which lid to use, or that both lids were the wrong ones for that particular bowl. Rather she merely observed Collette's exploration strategies in trying the two lids on the bowl, supporting the toddler's experimentation at her own imprecise level. When Collette walked away, Mena accepted that decision

as an approximation of the real and correct solution, knowing that Collette would return to the problem many times in the future and would adjust her decision about which lid fit a particular bowl. Making note of this event would remind Mena to check again in a few days to see how Collette was progressing in her work with bowls and lids.

Mena made the decision to carry out these supportive actions without speaking to Collette at all. She merely watched, listened, and smiled at the work Collette was doing in figuring out and solving the problem as she perceived it. If Collette had expressed frustration, Mena might have scaffolded her exploration. For an older toddler or preschooler, there might have been a conversation about the problem solving that was happening, but speaking is not always necessary when children are deeply engaged in their work. Indeed, adults easily can interfere with a child's plan and derail their thinking. Knowing when to watch and when to intervene is a learned skill.

Knowing when to add or remove materials is also a challenge and may differ for the children in the group. Mena could support Collette further by documenting her actions so that changes in Collette's thinking and understanding of space would become part of her learning record.

Contents and Containers With Infants

Many infants spend their waking hours in bouncy chairs or car seats. These containers (!) support the infants as they sit upright and observe their surroundings. However, they may delay children's physical development for sitting on their own. When possible, children benefit from floor time. Cushions may support young infants in different ways. Placing an infant on their tummy on a thin cushion will gently elevate their head and upper body so that the child can view the floor nearby. Interesting objects placed nearby will generate interest even if the child cannot reach them. Cushioning also may be used for infants who are able to sit upright but need support to keep them upright as well as protect them if they lose their balance. These infants can explore objects placed near their feet or in their laps. Adults also may support young infants who are seated on the floor or on the educator's lap. This allows the educator to observe more closely what the child is doing, which objects are most attractive, or whether the child is tiring and needs a change of position or activity.

Contents and Containers experiences for infants begin with their exploration of physical characteristics. As Piaget and Inhelder (1967) told us, these youngest children are checking for a variety of physical characteristics of objects in order to begin their construction of how the objects fit in the space around us. They can do this only by having access to many safe but interesting objects, including typical infant toys, household objects, natural materials, and materials with a variety of textures. Educators must be sure to include materials that provide more than visual stimulation so that any physical disabilities will be addressed.

Immobile infants must rely on the educators to supply objects within reach, or even hold the object while the infant touches it, if the infant is not yet able to grasp it successfully. During these experiences, educators may supply the names of the objects as well as descriptive terms. Educators may introduce objects inside containers so that the infants can explore rattling sounds, experience the visual stimulation of objects moving inside, or even watch an adult place an object inside a container and remove it repeatedly while saying "in" or "out." When educators verbalize their actions, it draws the infant's attention to what is being done and introduces spatial vocabulary that the infant can build on later. This can be carried out easily during normal routines. In this example, Amara uses the spatial language "empty," "in," "more room," and "full."

Textbox 5.3. Infants Explore Objects

Amara was sitting on the floor holding 6-month-old Aiden in her lap. Amara noticed that Aiden was looking at the sound basket (a basket filled with rattles and other objects that make sound when shaken) on the floor in front of them. As Amara moved to reach for one of the objects, her foot hit the basket and all the objects fell out. Aiden looked at Amara and then back to the now empty basket. Amara said, "Oh no! Now the basket is empty." She continued verbalizing, as she put each object back, one at a time. After each one she said, "I put the rattle IN the basket. Look [she tilted the basket so Aiden could see what was inside]. There is still more room. I think I'll put another one in."

She continued this until she ran out of objects. Then she said, "I wonder if we have room for more things." Another educator in the room placed several more objects on the floor near Amara and Aiden. Amara continued to put them in the basket, commenting after each one using the words "in" and "more room." As she placed the last object in the basket, she commented, "I think the basket is FULL. There is no more room."

In this example, we can see evidence of Amara incorporating both the ITM and ITILM. She observed Aiden's interest in the basket, and when she accidentally tipped it over, she made the decision to support deeper thinking by verbalizing what she was doing. She used her words to help Aiden strategize as she refilled the basket. Her words provided the opportunity to problem-solve, and she supported spatial learning through the words she chose to use.

Once infants can crawl or scoot to reach objects, their opportunities are expanded. They more easily can choose which objects to examine, although educators will notice these mobile infants using many of the same strategies to explore as the younger infants use. Grasping skills also increase opportunities to examine objects and move them around. The anecdote that begins this chapter demonstrates how Hadley, a nonwalking infant, still spent time with contents and containers, examining the ways she and the materials interacted. For these children, containers or contents are best if they are easy to grasp, such as the handle on the colander.

ITM: Engaging Infants. Once the infants are awake, engaging their interest is not difficult if materials are accessible and interesting. Most of the containers we used were transparent or translucent plastic. We found the initial interest level for all ages was highest and was maintained best if the children could see through the containers and see what was inside. This is especially the case for young infants who may not yet have an understanding of object permanence and may think that once you can no longer see an object it no longer exists.

From birth, children demonstrate a natural curiosity about their environments, including people. Educators of older children often plan introductory activities to spark interest. These are not needed for very young children, as they are not yet experts on anything in their world. They willingly explore any new materials within reach. Educators easily can capitalize on the infants' natural curiosity by allowing them to explore using a variety of senses so that they can watch objects move, listen to the sounds the objects make, and feel, smell, or taste the objects to explore their surfaces, tastes, and textures. These interactions require the educators to spend time with the infants in order to interact and to notice the children's responses to objects. In many settings, this is a challenge to do one-on-one. However, if possible, the ability to interact personally with each infant is important to the educator's understanding of that child's growth and development. These personal interactions also provide vital information for recording growth and development.

ITM: Providing Opportunities. Educators can facilitate exploration by offering contents that provide a variety of textures, shapes, colors, and sizes. Multiples of similar objects will support the interest level, especially for toddlers, but also are important for infants. Educators need to be alert to quantities of contents, however, so that children are not overwhelmed by too many objects. Educators may demonstrate different ways to interact with objects for these very young children. Infants have their own set of strategies once they can grasp objects. But adults may hold up objects and shake them gently, especially if objects inside make a noise or move inside the containers. For infants beginning to grasp, the adult can move the object closer and wait for the infant to grasp it.

Using materials already in the room as contents with a simple addition of containers can spark exploring in new ways. Knowing the children well will provide educators a sense of the appropriate set of objects for a particular child, as will alertness to the infant's change in interest due to hunger or fatigue.

A first consideration is always safety. Objects that are too small present choking hazards. Even objects that do not fit into a choke tube can be dangerous. Being observant not only provides opportunities for documenting growth and development, but also is vital for keeping the children safe. Educators need to regularly examine materials throughout the environment to be sure that only the best materials are available to the children. Cracked or broken plastic items should be removed and discarded immediately.

Some plastic household items that are designed for adult use may have fairly sharp edges that need to be covered or the items removed entirely. Containers may contain objects or liquids inside to view but not manipulate; these containers should be glued or securely taped shut.

Adults differ in their verbal interactions with infants. Some of us provide a running commentary on our own actions as well as the infant's actions. Others ask questions about what the child is experiencing or thinking. For this youngest age group, we don't expect answers, but asking the questions is part of the serve-and-return approach to providing a responsive environment and fostering communication. Keeping comments and questions simple will provide conversation without overwhelming the infant. Naming objects and actions as they occur, using self-talk to describe your own actions, or using parallel talk to describe the child's actions also will provide a foundation for the adult–child relationship. And sometimes, saying nothing is the best choice of all.

ITM: Making Decisions. Educators of infants continually are making decisions in providing care for infants. Is it time to change their diaper? Are they hungry or tired? Is the infant warm enough? To answer these questions, educators may gather information and often keep documentation, such as times that diapers were changed, time of feeding and amount taken, or time and length of naps.

This same approach can be used when making decisions about what materials to provide, when to change materials, and more. Just as notes are taken for caregiving routines, educators can take notes for materials, actions, and times an infant explores and plays. These notes can serve as documentation of learning and shared with parents. If possible, photos along with the notes provide a way to share what the infant did and serve as a way to document an infant's development over time. A simple photo of a child reaching for an object and attempting to grasp it, with a simple note of the date, gives educators and parents a view of the infant's growing ability and interest. It also helps in making decisions on what to do next to support the infant's developmental abilities and interests. What materials can be added? What might parents do at home to support this? This type of documentation can be posted in the room for the infants to look at and for the educators to review.

Taking notes on young infants' interests and actions will support the educator's understanding of the child's development. As infants develop control of their head and are able to reach for but not grasp objects, observe them to see what things they look at longer or attempt to reach for, or what things cause them to move arms and legs in excitement. Mobile infants are more able to demonstrate their interests. Educators can note what objects the infants move toward, pick up, and examine. Make note of the actions they perform on the objects.

Observations also will support an educator's assessment of whether a child may be signaling a potential physical disability. Records of anecdotes of the child's actions can be shared with parents or other colleagues to identify when a child needs additional services or assessment.

Contents and Containers With Young Toddlers

Young toddlers, such as Collette, whom we discussed in the anecdote above, enjoy exploring materials in a variety of ways. When we first introduced the tubs of plastic containers, the toddlers spent time each day examining the different sizes and shapes of objects, sometimes just throwing the containers to the floor as they lifted them out of the large tubs (see Figure 5.3).

Figure 5.3. A Young Toddler Checks Out the Lid

After only a few days, they began to examine the different containers more closely, choosing the materials they wanted to explore, and locating objects to place inside the containers. Both young and older toddlers spent an hour each day exploring these materials for at least 5 weeks. The amount and variety of the materials provided many different opportunities so that the children did not appear to tire of them. Allowing the young toddlers to choose the materials they wanted to use appeared to increase their interest and persistence in finding and solving problems.

Young toddlers are expanding their ideas about space and what fits where. Canister sets of three or four provide good opportunities for this when combined with plastic balls of different sizes and colors, such as those found in ball pits. Young toddlers engage in pouring and filling these canisters over and over, learning how many balls fit or don't. Muffin tins of varying sizes also provide interesting containers for these same balls. These toddlers expressed frustration when they ran out of balls before filling the muffin tins, so having enough balls available to completely fill the muffin tins is important. It also is important to observe young toddlers as they engage with the materials. Using the ITILM can help the educator understand the child's actions.

Textbox 5.4. Layering Materials

Sheri, 14 months old, worked alone in a quiet corner. She selected a yellow ball and a container of sheer scarves from the shelf. She carefully wrapped a ball inside a scarf, then placed the wrapped ball into one cup of a muffin tin. She continued wrapping balls with scarves until she ran out of scarves.

In her work, Sheri used the balls as contents and the scarves as containers. Then she used the wrapped balls as contents and the muffin tin as a container. In this process she engaged in both strategizing and resolving. She combined strategies in wrapping the balls and then placing them inside the muffin tin. She created this interesting combination, which was more complex than simply placing the balls in the muffin tin. Sheri repeated this process on other days, seeming to find satisfaction with this way to use the materials. She appeared to have planned how she would use the materials before she began. This layering of materials was a form of nesting that we had not considered in our own experiences with the materials (see Figure 5.4).

Educators also can create simple, but interesting, materials from a variety of household containers. One example is a tube-shaped oatmeal container. One educator glued family photographs around the outside of an oatmeal tube, one tube for each child, and then allowed the children to use the container to hold their choice of contents. The photos encouraged the children to rotate the containers to see all the photos of their own family, supporting both motor development and their understanding that the box had more than one side to view, as well as being a holder for chosen objects.

Young toddlers also will begin to consider how their bodies fit in space. If one young toddler climbs into the large tub, you can be sure that others will do that as well. Recognizing that a container is large enough to hold your entire body is part of the learning, because some containers are large enough for only a hand or a head or a foot. Adults will need to consider whether this activity is suitable for their setting. We experienced some educators who were not concerned when toddlers climbed inside the tubs, while other educators did not allow this at all.

In contrast, some young toddlers chose to carry multiple objects using only their bodies and clothing as the container. The children devised ways to interact with materials that we had not considered. They slid objects into pockets if they had them, carried objects under their arms, or squeezed objects into the front of their stomachs, using their arms to keep the objects there. In these cases, the toddlers' bodies became the containers for a variety of contents. They often carried them around the room, dumped them, and left to find more of the same object. Educators are encouraged to let children move materials from place to place during this type of exploration. When the child loses interest or playtime is over, then the child can be guided to return the materials to the tub.

ITM: Engaging Young Toddlers. Young toddlers, unlike infants who are not yet mobile, are able to move to the things that interest them and are able to grasp and manipulate materials on their own. As long as the educator has provided a variety of safe, interesting materials that are easily accessible to young toddlers, the young toddlers will engage with them. Educators may begin with the same kinds of materials described for young infants and add other materials as the toddlers become more engaged. We recommend providing enough materials so that children do not need to compete for an item that is especially interesting.

ITM: Providing Opportunities. In addition to providing safe and interesting materials for the children to explore, the educator needs to plan time for exploration to take place. We have observed young toddlers engage with materials, walk away, and return later to continue their exploration. This exploration is often a type of problem solving the young toddler engages in, and allowing materials to stay out for long periods of time gives children the chance to return to the problem to explore new solutions or repeat actions they tried before.

ITM: Making Decisions. Once the children are engaged with the materials, the educator can observe

Figure 5.4. Sheri Wraps the Balls

what the children are doing and document it. This documentation can be notes the educator makes while observing or can be photographs of the child and the materials. Often there is no need to intervene with young toddlers unless there is a safety issue or a child is showing frustration. After observing, the educator can decide whether there are changes that need to be made. For example, in the case of Sheri noted above, the educator may decide to add more scarves or other types of cloth for Sheri to explore the next day.

Muffin tins remained an attraction throughout our study of contents and containers (see Figure 5.5). On occasion, the toddlers would engage in pretend play using the muffin tins and contents, although this did not seem to interrupt their explorations of spatial relationships. The actions of the older toddlers became more sophisticated after substantial experience with the materials, and they used materials in unexpected ways. We also noted the differences in knowledge construction among these older toddlers, whose attention to the details of materials may vary

Figure 5.5. Filling the Muffin Tin

widely from child to child. This may be due to prior experiences or differences in development between toddlers. In any case, the muffin tins appeared to attract both young and older toddlers for a variety of explorations.

Contents and Containers With Older Toddlers

Older toddlers are thinking about things in different ways than infants and younger toddlers. Because of the variety of personal experiences and families, some older toddlers seem to be more advanced in their thinking than others. Educators of infants and toddlers are often the first to experience these differences in learning.

TEXTBOX 5.5. MANAGING THE BALLS IN A MUFFIN TIN

Jacob and Cho Wei, both 32 months old, were seated on the floor. Jacob began to place balls into a 12-cup, medium-size muffin tin. Jacob used two different-sized balls without watching how the balls fit in the cups. Cho Wei was watching closely. He noticed that if two large balls were in adjacent cups, one of the balls would rise up slightly and move to the side, lifting partially out of the cup. These large balls were too large for the muffin cups. Cho Wei moved a smaller ball into the adjacent cup, which let the large ball sit solidly in the cup. Each time Jacob placed two large balls in adjacent cups, Cho Wei would make the switch so that all the balls formed a checkerboard-like ABAB pattern of big ball, small ball. This continued across the face of the entire muffin tin. Jacob did not notice either the problem of placing two large balls adjacently or his friend correcting the ball placement so that the balls all fit well. Cho Wei smiled at his arrangement of balls.

If we had not observed this as it occurred, we would not have noticed that Cho Wei was producing a pattern with the balls placed in the muffin tin. If he had carried the finished collection to show an educator, they may not have noticed the pattern because it was not obviously developed with the balls' colors. Taking the time to observe how children work with materials provides many new opportunities for educators to challenge their understanding of the learning that is taking place.

Cho Wei's actions with the balls in the muffin tin demonstrate how he engaged in inquiry, as described in the ITILM. His wonder began when he carefully watched Jacob placing the balls in the muffin tin. As he watched, he discovered a problem when two large balls were placed together. He strategized by replacing one of the large balls with a smaller ball, and he observed how that action worked so that both balls sank down into the muffin cup. When he realized that his actions solved the problem, he continued replacing the large balls with small balls as needed. Once the muffin tin was full, Cho Wei smiled, indicating he was satisfied with his solution. He had resolved the problem. By engaging in this inquiry experience, Cho Wei not only found a satisfying solution, but also learned that he could use his own ideas and actions to solve problems.

ITM: Engaging Older Toddlers. Just as with infants and younger toddlers, it is important to provide safe and interesting materials for the children to explore. Older toddlers, like Cho Wei, may engage in more complex explorations. This more complex exploration is more likely to happen if the educator provides a greater variety of materials and allows ample time for free play with those materials. This may mean having the materials out for longer time periods during the day as well as having them available for several days. Educators can observe to note when children lose interest in some materials, and those materials can be removed and replaced with new objects.

ITM: Providing Opportunities. Much of what educators do is the same as what they do with infants and young toddlers; however, older toddlers are much more independent and are able to verbalize. Educators still need to observe carefully, but now they also can have the children's words give insight into their thinking. Educators may want to take photos of children and display the photos along with the words the children said. Older toddlers are able to look at the photos and be reminded of what they were doing. This often leads to further exploration of the materials, supporting development of more complex spatial skills.

Matias, 30 months old, was standing by Erin, an educator who was sitting on the floor. He held a small clear container. He pushed a red plastic pit ball into the container, and then tried to take it out. He tried pulling it out, but it wouldn't budge. He then tried tipping the container over, but the ball stayed stuck. Matias approached Erin, showing her the container with the ball stuck inside. Erin had been observing Matias and responded to his gesture by saying, "I know. It's stuck. Now what can you do?" She made decisions by intervening to help Matias think deeper to find a solution. At the same time, she provided opportunities for Matias to problem-solve on his own, with her nearby to intervene if needed.

Matias walked away as he shook the container with the open end facing up. He stopped shaking and looked inside to see that the ball was still there. He touched the ball and tried to grasp it to pull it out but realized his hand could not fit around the ball. Erin observed but continued to let Matias try on his own. He tried shaking it again, more vigorously, and the ball finally popped out and fell to the floor. Matias exclaimed, "I got it out!" Erin responded, "See, you figured it out." Matias immediately inserted the ball into the container again, and the ball was again stuck. He used his former strategy of shaking, but the ball didn't move. Erin asked, "How can you get it out now?," and Matias responded, "I don't know." Erin engaged the learner by asking Matias, "What did you do last time?" Matias then shook the container, reached in and tried to grasp the ball, and returned to shaking. He stopped, looked at the ball in the container, then set the container on the shelf and walked away. At the time he was content to leave the problem. Erin knew that Matias might return to this problem later but realized he might need a break. She left the materials where they were so the opportunity to return to the problem was still available to Matias.

This example of Matias and Erin shows how an educator can use the ITM to support inquiry during the normal routines of the schedule. Erin did not have a preplanned activity to encourage Matias to explore the size relationship of the ball and the container or to teach problem solving. This happened during free play, and Erin capitalized on Matias's natural curiosity. She now has evidence of Matias's developing spatial concepts and perseverance. To document this, she can make notes or, if possible, capture a photo.

ITM: Making Decisions. These additional insights will foster communication between educators and with parents about children's growth and development. Educators will become more creative in adding materials that spark interest and encourage children's explorations. Educators also will have a better foundation of understanding about each child's developmental abilities, recognizing when a child appears to need additional assistance in particular developmental domains.

As we noted in Chapter 3, educators make many decisions throughout the day. Some are routine, but others require consideration of the situation. Providing new materials to very young children may lead to conflicts, frustration, and a messy classroom. Educators who choose to embrace inquiry learning and teaching will place the children at the forefront of decision-making. This primary decision then will lead to the need to explain the situation to administrators, fellow educators, assistants, parents, visitors, or other family members.

EDUCATOR PLANNING FOR CONTENTS AND CONTAINERS

Most of the containers we suggest are inexpensive storage containers available from many stores or online. Educators may search their home kitchens for containers or ask parents or other family members to donate a variety. Objects to be used as contents may come from typical classroom materials, or specific ones may be selected by educators. We found that children will seek out specific contents themselves. Observing their actions also may spark ideas for educators about what additional materials might be interesting and engaging. We were surprised by some of the materials that intrigued the toddlers. Many of them spent considerable time zipping and unzipping the plastic envelopes we found or recycled for storing materials (see Figure 5.6).

Figure 5.6. Zipping and Unzipping

Hair rollers were another surprise, with the bonus that they nest perfectly! Storing contents and containers in large tubs allows for easy access for the children during center or playtime.

Educators must be on guard to inspect plastic items regularly and remove any cracked or broken materials to avoid injury or choking on pieces. Materials should be cleaned regularly as well, because many children will be mouthing items.

We observed children engaged with contents and containers over several weeks for an hour each day. The children remained interested in the materials and continued to explore their own ways of using the containers and finding interesting contents. That short attention span assigned to toddlers never appeared. We know from this experience that providing interesting materials and plenty of time allows children to engage in inquiry learning. We also learned that our role as educators was enhanced as we used the Inquiry Teaching Model as a guide for observing, documenting, and supporting that inquiry learning.

CHAPTER 6

Chutes and Silos: Spatial Relationships and Problem Solving With Infants and Toddlers

Rosemary Geiken and Sherri Peterson

Landon was a "frequent flyer" in STEM experiences that were launched in his young toddler classroom. When the Chutes and Silos materials were introduced, he was one of the first toddlers to join the educator in the area where the tubes and balls were placed (see Figure 6.1).

Figure 6.1. Landon Drags a Bag of Materials

TEXTBOX 6.1. LANDON DRAGS A BAG

Landon was particularly interested in the mesh bag in which the tubes were stored. He loosened the string at the top and then tipped the bag and shook it until the tubes were all on the floor. He then tried to get one long, skinny tube back in the bag. When he was unsuccessful after multiple attempts, he said, "Help you," while looking at one of the educators. She said, "Landon, would you like me to help you put the tube in?" When he nodded his head, she modeled the sign for "help" and assisted him to place the tube into the bag. He carried it to the climber and dragged it up the stairs and around the corner to the ramp on the other side with some difficulty. He found that the bag was stuck sideways in the opening to the ramp. He pulled on it and repositioned it so that he could drag it down the ramp. When he reached the bottom of the ramp, he turned around and tried to carry it up the ramp. When he found that it was again lodged in the opening, he made several attempts to pull it through. When he was unable to move it, he dropped the string at the top of the bag handle and stepped over the bag, up the ramp, and down the stairs, where he picked up the string handle and pulled the bag around the room.

Later he approached the stairs again where another child had dropped a tube. He stepped on the tube, tried to balance on top of it, and slid off the tube. He continued to practice his balancing skills several more times before moving to another tube.

On a subsequent day, Landon began using the tubes as a container for the new wooden block people that had been added to the block center. He started by filling a long tube with the wooden people. When it was filled, he turned to another tube that was larger in diameter, but not as long, and added block people to that tube. When the block people did not go into the tube easily, he rotated or flipped them so they would drop in.

When he had filled the tube with people, he picked it up as if to move it and was surprised when the contents spilled out of the open bottom of the tube. He began to pick them up and add them to the tube until it was full. He was engaged in this self-initiated experience for nearly 10 minutes.

Landon continued his investigation with tubes and contents during another center time with a bag full of foam blocks of various sizes that had been added to the Chutes and Silos center. When he saw the new materials, he took them out of the bag and stacked and organized them on a low table before he moved to the tubes. He selected a long blue tube and began to fill it with cylindrical blocks. He held the tube with one hand while he placed blocks inside and tipped the tube carefully while reaching to get more blocks so that the blocks did not slide from the bottom of the tube. When he had filled the tube several times, he emptied it, moved the tube over a block, and tapped it so that he could "capture" one of the blocks with the bottom of the tube. When he had finished filling the tubes with blocks, he picked up two long tubes and used them as walking sticks as he left the area.

During the time that the chutes and silos were available to Landon, he varied his investigations as he increased his understanding about the possibilities within the activity. He filled tubes with many materials, including colorful sheer scarves, squishy and rigid balls of various sizes, foam and wooden blocks, and both human-made and natural materials from around the room, including some seashells he found with the loose parts. He tipped, rolled, filled, captured, and experimented with sounds that could be made when he used his voice inside the tube. He sorted by size and color, experimented with the position of the tube as he moved balls back and forth inside, and considered how he could change the size of the squishy balls by squeezing in order to make them fit in the narrower tubes. He demonstrated initiative and curiosity and his increasing competence as he used interesting materials that engaged

Figure 6.2. Landon Fills a Tube

his senses and provided opportunities for himself to practice his developing motor skills and make mental connections. He continually posed problems for himself and persisted until he solved them to his satisfaction.

WHY CHUTES AND SILOS WITH INFANTS AND TODDLERS?

Chutes and Silos is a physical science activity involving clear acrylic tubes (http://www.safespaceconcepts .com/ToolsForDiscovery.html) with colored edging or caps on the end. These edges and caps provide a safety feature for very young children. They are used with a variety of objects such as balls, cylinders, natural materials, and found objects for infants and toddlers to explore by filling, emptying, nesting, sorting, collecting, tipping, rolling, carrying, capturing, and comparing (Geiken, 2011). The materials appeal to children's interests, their fascination with figuring out how the physical world works, and their desire to modify it to make something interesting happen.

In Landon's classroom, the selection of interesting materials for the toddlers provided multiple opportunities for them to explore the properties and functions of objects. The purpose of the materials is to nurture the development of dispositions that we find are evident when infants and toddlers engage in STEM experiences, such as identifying problems, making predictions, using tools, designing and creating, and building things that work.

Infant Toddler Inquiry Learning Model With Chutes and Silos

In these observations of Landon's actions with the Chutes and Silos materials, we saw evidence of his wonder as he investigated these new materials that were introduced in his classroom. His experiences with other STEM learning centers, such as Contents and Containers, exploring water, and play in the block center, had allowed him to build the basis for inquiry, analysis, and logical thought.

His exploration of the new materials demonstrated this nonlinear process that we see with infant and toddler inquiry. He moved freely from wonder, to strategizing, to resolution, and then additional strategizing, wondering, and resolution, during our observations. Landon investigated the materials, although not the materials his educators predicted that he would find the most intriguing or in the way they had expected he might investigate them. His interest in dumping, filling, and hauling the mesh bag was a revelation to Landon's educators, even though they had observed his innovations with other STEM learning centers. They had investigated the materials, prepared the environment, and strategized about the possibilities within the materials. Their planning did not include specific lessons to be taught. Rather, they kept in mind what they knew about how toddlers learn and the scope and sequence of children's development in this age range, and then opened themselves up to the possibilities using selective intervention based on their knowledge about individual children and their learning dispositions.

In these observations of Landon's explorations of the materials, we saw him continue to gain knowledge about the properties of the chutes and silos when he developed the new strategy of positioning the tubes in a specific way so that the blocks did not slip out of the bottom of the tube as the block people had when he used them as contents for the tubes. We also saw him carefully selecting only the cylindrical foam blocks to fill his tube. We can only guess at his thinking about shape, but wondered whether he chose cylinders because of the tube design. During several of the Chutes and Silos play experiences that educators documented, Landon demonstrated problem solving as he repeated his actions with the materials several times and then stopped as if thinking about his next action before repeating it or trying a new strategy.

The length of time he needed to develop a new strategy varied over the time he investigated the materials. He often would use an old strategy as he played, walk away to engage in another activity, and then use the materials again, sometimes with a new strategy. Throughout the time that chutes and silos were available, Landon continued to engage with the materials. His educators added new materials to use with the tubes and placed them in different parts of the classroom in order to engage all children in the center. Landon repeatedly found new and interesting materials in the classroom and carried them to the Chutes and Silos center. In his classroom, this kind of exploration was part of the classroom culture, and educators trusted children to pose their own questions and find answers in their own way and in their own time.

Inquiry Teaching Model With Chutes and Silos

The environment in Landon's toddler classroom was a thoughtful balance that is safe yet allows the children to have interesting experiences that inspire their curiosity and initiative. The educators observed children's actions and provided selective intervention based on their understanding of each child's approaches to learning, prior experiences, motor development, and persistence.

Infants and toddlers need to explore and make sense of the world, and "have the capacity to become deeply engaged" (Lewin-Benham, 2010, p. 9). Within their exploration, they repeat actions many times in order to understand. Open-ended materials like those within Chutes and Silos are important because they allow many approaches and stimulate long engagement. In *More Than a Foundation: Young Children Are Capable STEM Learners*, McClure (2017) stated, "When we say children are 'born scientists,' we're not just being cute; they really are active scientists, right now, systematically and intentionally exploring their environments, even from the day they are born" (p. 83).

While science exploration might come naturally to most infants and toddlers, there are huge intellectual benefits when adults nurture the natural scientist. Adults deepen STEM learning when they support young children's pursuit of new understandings, foster excitement for learning, and engage children in experiences that stimulate their brains and grow their sensory and motor systems. Adults can build and expand on young children's scientific interest when they (1) are aware of children's developmental levels and previous experiences; (2) have investigated the materials before introducing them to children; (3) allow time for infants' and toddlers' exploration and problem solving; and (4) interact with them as they investigate carefully selected materials.

Chutes and Silos Experiences With Infants

Jonathon approached the chutes and silos the educators had added near the carpeted area of his infant classroom. His educators knew that he would be one of the first of the infants to investigate these new materials. His interest in balls and things that he could move, throw, roll, spin, and bounce had been evident since he began to gain more control of his actions. He was a skilled creeper and crawler and was beginning to pull to stand and cruise low furniture. His fine-motor skills enabled him to grasp, pinch, rotate, squeeze, and release objects of various sizes. Jonathon began his investigation by seating himself near a mesh bag filled with differently sized blue plastic pit balls and one of the larger tubes. He picked up each ball and slid it into the tube that he had positioned on his leg

so that it was tilted slightly (see Figure 6.3). He continued to slide balls into the tube one at a time without noticing that they were sliding out of the bottom of the tube. When all the balls from the bag had been used, he retrieved some that had rolled out of the tube and began sliding them into the tube again. This time the balls were sliding out more quickly, as the tube had shifted when he moved. Jonathon noticed that they were spilling onto the floor and moved so that he could reach the balls. He repeated this several times with varying results as the tube moved to different positions on his leg.

ITM: Engaging Infants. Infants learn by acting on objects, with a natural curiosity and wonder about the world and all things in it. Educators can capitalize on this natural curiosity by engaging infants with interesting and open-ended materials. In this

Figure 6.3. Filling a Tube With Balls

example with Jonathon, the educators activated his prior knowledge and experiences by setting out a few of the tubes, a variety of balls, and other objects, including scarves, blocks, and small toys.

The educators identified his interest in balls of any kind in their observations and documentation from previous STEM investigations and by noticing the toys and materials that he selected from the shelves in the classroom. In their regular communication with his family, they learned that he and his older brother enjoyed participating in rough-and-tumble play involving pit balls, playground balls, and soft balls with their cousins and neighborhood friends. As he engaged with the materials, his educator made comments based on his actions and offered a few simple questions: "Look how tall that is. I wonder how you got those balls in there?" or, "You have the big ball. I wonder if you can hold a big ball and a little ball?"

Educators can use comments and questions to suggest rather than lead infants into a particular activity. If the infant does not respond to a suggestion, educators can move on to another comment or question. They also may want to model for the infant while making comments about what they are doing. "I put the small blue ball in the tube. It rolled down the tube and onto the floor." By modeling and commenting on the infants' actions, educators help them label objects and construct their knowledge of the physical world. This is a time to be intentional about adding new materials when the infants have fully explored the initial offering. Including some objects that fit into the tubes, and some that do not fit provides multiple opportunities for problem solving.

ITM: Providing Opportunities. Educators of infants can provide opportunities by setting up an environment of "yes," where exploration can occur without restrictions on movement because the materials are safe and provide multiple options for exploration, problem solving, and vocabulary development. When infants discover a bag of clear tubes and balls in a variety of sizes in a corner of their classroom, they are invited to explore the possibilities with the support of the educators. Some older infants, like Jonathon, will grab the tubes and balls to begin investigating with enthusiasm and will require very little intervention from the educator as they discover the many possibilities that these materials offer. Younger

infants who are not yet able to sit independently will require more assistance with their investigation of chutes and silos. They may lie near the tubes and roll them back and forth, or simply find a squishy ball that can be squeezed, dropped endlessly onto the floor, or popped into their mouth.

Creepers, crawlers, and scooters will find the cylindrical tubes appealing as they travel across the floor of the classroom and attend to the movement of the tubes. They will use the tubes as containers by stuffing toys and balls inside or as noisemakers when they tap the tubes on the floor or table or knock them together. They may discover new perspectives as the tubes and contents roll across the floor. Educators can foster communication by commenting on children's actions, describing what they are observing, or naming the materials.

ITM: Making Decisions. Educators can make informed decisions when they create detailed notes, take photos, or videotape children's response to the materials introduced in STEM investigations. Sharing documentation with the teaching team in order to reflect on children's actions during the experience can assist educators in making decisions about what's next for the children in their classroom. Documentation may provide more questions than answers for reflective educators.

In Jonathon's classroom, the educators made a decision to use blue pit balls in three different sizes so that they could observe the problem-solving actions of the children more carefully. By eliminating other variables within the materials, the educators could document Jonathon's actions as he tried to fit the different-sized balls into the different-sized tubes. In the following days, they added other balls that could be used with the tubes, including some that fit in none of the tubes and some soft balls that could be squeezed to alter the size. This kind of careful honing of materials can assist educators of young children to really see the actions of children and to prepare the environment more thoughtfully for future STEM experiences. When this documentation is shared with families, it can provide powerful messages about the learning that is taking place and offer educators and families very specific information about individual children and their learning progression.

Chutes and Silos Experiences With Young Toddlers

TEXTBOX 6.3 ARIANNA FILLS A TUBE

Arianna joined the other children who had gathered near the center where their educator had placed some mesh bags filled with clear tubes and interesting objects, including foam blocks and plastic pit balls. She played beside Landon as he stacked and sorted the blocks according to their attributes and then went to another area of the classroom. She returned to the Chutes and Silos center and noticed the tubes standing upright near the sensory table. She picked up a block, inspected it carefully, and then dropped it inside the tube. She repeated her actions several times before noticing that the blocks were dropping out of the bottom of the tube. She retrieved them and placed them on the table. Arianna left to play with peers in another center and returned to find that the tubes had been left lying on the floor. She lay down on the floor to examine the tubes more closely, rolled them back and forth, then placed a cylindrical foam block inside one of the tubes as it lay on the floor. She paused to inspect the result of her actions and began stuffing the tube with identical blocks. She added blocks to the tube until it was filled to the opening. She inspected the tube, noticed that there was room at the opposite end of the tube for more blocks, and placed her arm inside the tube to push the blocks further down into the tube. She continued to add only cylindrical blocks until she was satisfied that there were "enough" blocks in the tube. She shook the tube so that the blocks moved back and forth inside, then stood and placed the tube on end. She lifted the tube and watched as the foam blocks slipped out onto the floor (see Figure 6.4).

ITM: *Engaging Young Toddlers.* Young toddlers easily are engaged with chutes and silos. Their first investigations will look like their first explorations of the materials used with contents and containers or other materials. They will dump the balls and tubes out of the bags and tubs where the materials are stored; fill the tubes with balls, blocks, or other materials they find in the classroom (see Figure 6.4); and may be more interested in the bags and tubs than in the materials themselves. As the children have more time with the tubes and balls, educators may want

Figure 6.4. Arianna Fills a Tube

to offer additional materials. Arianna's investigation of the foam blocks and tube occurred after she had engaged with the tubes and balls over several days.

As toddlers begin to fill the tubes with objects, they will be surprised when they lift the tubes and find that all the objects roll or slide out of the bottom of the tube. They will fill the tubes many times before they begin to make a connection between their actions and the result. We noticed that this resulted because the children concentrated on the top of the tube rather than noticing both the top and bottom, something Piaget (1954) called *centration*—focus centered on one thing at a time. Educators can support young children in this process by making comments or asking simple questions that will engage the toddlers in thinking about what is happening. Including one or two tubes with closed bottoms can encourage strategizing about the problem of keeping the balls contained. As the toddlers engage with the materials, educators can activate prior knowledge and capitalize on the toddlers' natural curiosity with careful observations that will inform them when new materials might be needed.

ITM: *Providing Opportunities.* After children have had some time with the materials, educators can encourage further investigation by intentionally offering just a few of the materials for investigation. When educators select tubes of different sizes, balls that will go through all the tubes, and balls that will go through only some of them, toddlers will have the opportunity to focus on the physical features of the tubes and balls. Making comments or asking productive questions such as, "What can you do with these? I wonder what will happen if you put the big yellow ball into the red tube? Is there a way to get all the blue balls out of the tube? Look what happened when you . . . ," can provide additional opportunities for strategizing with the materials. Educators can foster communication by identifying the tubes and balls with very specific labels. Helping toddlers to categorize by shape, color, length, diameter, or other descriptors can support children's thinking about the relationships between the materials. For instance, if the educator had commented on Landon's actions with the foam blocks, Arianna may have noticed that he was sorting them by shape, size, and color. The educator could have commented, "Landon, you have all of the blocks that are shaped like cylinders in a group. The cylinders are the same shape as the tubes." Arianna may have used the cylindrical foam blocks purely by coincidence, but she may have been paying attention to Landon's work. Educators who observe closely over multiple play sessions will have the opportunity to learn amazing things about the capabilities of the toddlers in the classroom.

ITM: *Making Decisions.* Information gathered by observing young toddlers as they engage with materials gives educators evidence that is essential in order to make informed decisions about what children need. Identifying children's interests, documenting progress, and gathering input from others who know the children are an essential part of the decision-making process. Arianna's educators were surprised when they viewed the videotape of her tube exploration during their planned collaboration time. They were curious about her selection of cylindrically shaped blocks. They looked at the documentation that was gathered when Landon was sorting the blocks and at the footage of Arianna, and determined that they wanted more information about Arianna's understanding of the materials. They discussed their observations with her family to see what they were noticing at home and then offered materials in particular ways in order to observe and document her selection of materials.

This kind of informed decision-making is at the heart of the inquiry-based classroom. Educators who are intentional in their selection of materials, the manner in which materials are offered, and the interventions used to support young children as they investigate the materials are on the way to providing an inquiry-based learning environment. When this is done within the context of trusting relationships, educators can promote the development of initiative and curiosity, persistence with difficult tasks, focus and sustained attention, reasoning, and problem solving.

Chutes and Silos Experiences With Older Toddlers

The educators in a classroom with toddlers from 24–36 months introduced Chutes and Silos materials to their children, who investigated them over several weeks. Many of the children maintained their interest in the tubes and the other materials that were included in the center, but the educators had noticed that for some children interest was beginning to wane. They decided to introduce a large board covered with the loop side of hook and loop fabric, which they attached vertically to the back of a shelf unit. They attached the hook side of the fabric to tubes of various sizes so that the tubes could be attached to the board in different positions, including vertically, horizontally, or diagonally (see Figure 6.5). They also included some of the same balls, blocks, and other objects that had been used in the original Chutes and Silos investigation.

The toddlers quickly recognized the opportunities with this expansion of materials. They experimented with the fabric board first, sticking and unsticking tubes and enjoying the sound that accompanied their actions. Then they began to explore a wide variety of objects to see which would roll or slide through the tubes at various angles, and which would not move at all unless the angle of the tube was steeper.

Figure 6.5. Dropping Balls Through Tubes on the Velcro Wall

One of the tubes was open only at the top, so when the children placed balls and other objects into that tube, there was irregularity that provided a new opportunity for problem solving and the development of different strategies for using the tubes. Some older children began using this short, closed tube as a "catcher" for the balls that they were rolling down the tubes that had been placed vertically or at an angle on the hook and loop board. Younger toddlers often used a tub or other container with a wide mouth to catch balls as they fell through the tubes stuck on the wall.

it was vertical to the floor, placed his hand inside the tube, and tried to push the ball out the other end. He discovered that his arm was not long enough. He studied the problem and then began to tap the end of the tube on the floor. The ball moved a little further down the tube. When the ball stopped moving, he began pounding the tube on the floor. When he noticed that neither of these strategies was working, he asked Greta, one of the educators, for help. She tried to stick her hand into the tube to move the ball, but her hand didn't fit. She returned it to Tommy, who then rolled a smaller ball inside the tube to try to push the stuck ball out. He alternated between tapping and rolling, but the ball would not move. Greta suggested finding a tool that was long enough to push the ball out. She helped Tommy to search the classroom. They spied a kitchen scrubber with a long handle. Tommy grabbed the scrubber and shoved it into the tube, but it was not long enough to push the ball. Greta asked Tommy what else they might use, and he continued to search. They spied a yardstick in the kitchen, and she asked Tommy if he thought it might work. He grinned at her and stuck the yardstick into the tube. The yardstick went in easily and stopped in the space between the ball and the inside of the tube. Tommy moved it up and down for several minutes and the ball began to slide. Greta saw that his new strategy was not efficient and asked Tommy if there was another method he could use. Tommy continued using the same strategy of moving the yardstick up and down. When he saw the ball roll out of the tube he looked at Greta and said, "I did it!" (see Figure 6.6).

ITM: Engaging Older Toddlers. Older toddlers will be as intrigued as the infants and young toddlers when chutes and silos are introduced. Educators can set out a variety of tubes with blocks, balls, and other materials—some that fit in all the tubes and others that do not. Older toddlers may begin by putting objects inside the tubes to observe what happens. They may nest tubes and take them apart, noticing that one tube fits inside another. They will begin to notice similarities and differences in the objects and specifically select items based on their properties. Educators can support children's problem solving by asking productive questions as they add materials: "I wonder if you can get any more in there? What will

Figure 6.6. Problem Solving With Tubes

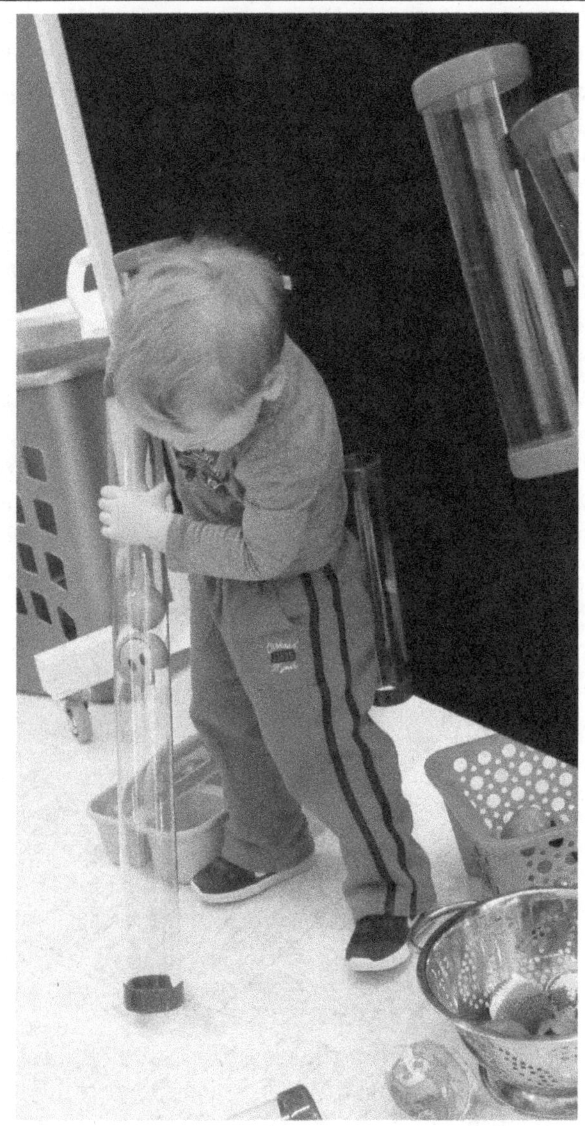

happen if you put the squishy ball in?" "I wonder if there is anything else you could try?" "What other balls do you have that might work in that one?" "Is there anything else you would like to try?" "That's a problem. Is there anything you can do to fix that?"

It is important for educators to use interventions selectively as they observe and document the investigation. Adults can disrupt a child's investigation by asking a question that the child is not ready for or that does not reflect their actions or goals. Narrating what the child is doing may be just the right amount of intervention for some children, while others simply may want the educator to demonstrate interest in what they are doing. Educators who encourage inquiry learning are mindful about whose agenda is the priority and save their intervention for a time when the child is becoming disengaged or uninterested. In the example with Tommy and his educator, there was clear evidence that Tommy had tried all of the strategies he had about dislodging the ball and was ready for Greta to intervene. She was able to provide him with support and then back off when it was clear that he was going to proceed with the strategy he had developed. Sometimes children's ideas are more effective than the ones an adult would choose. Sometimes children are committed to the strategy they have chosen even if it isn't working the way the adult believes that it should. Children sometimes find resolution to their self-imposed problems by walking away and trying it again later. As educators, it can be difficult to "zip our lips" and "sit on our hands" when children are solving problems they have selected. As with any new learning for adults or children, it will take practice.

ITM: Providing Opportunities. When young children select activities that are of interest to them, they are more likely to demonstrate sustained attention and motivation (Lewin-Benham, 2010). High-quality STEM experiences appeal to children's interest, inspire experimentation, and foster cooperation. When young children have the opportunity to explore and investigate, they begin to make connections, and these connections help them to make sense of the physical world. In the above example with Tommy and his educator, we see him engaged in a STEM experience that appealed to his interest and that inspired him to experiment. In his exploration with the tubes and balls, a problem developed that he was interested in solving. He persisted by using strategies that were familiar to him, such as pushing the ball with his arm and tapping the tube on the floor. His actions did not work to dislodge the ball but he persisted, trying these strategies several times. When he was unsuccessful, he was able to call upon a trusted adult to provide selective intervention so that he could develop a new strategy. This trusted adult had observed and documented his learning over time, so she understood Tommy's need for autonomy. She provided an opportunity for Tommy to make new connections with the materials and feel that sense of satisfaction when he was able to resolve the problem with the ball.

ITM: Making Decisions. By analyzing the difficulty of the experience and considering children's interests, educators will be prepared to (1) introduce materials with the right amount of challenge; (2) set up the environment to provide multiple opportunities for children to explore the properties and functions of objects; and (3) nurture the development of STEM learning dispositions. In these examples, we saw educators recognize when children were ready for a new challenge based on their observations and documentation. The adults collaborated on a strategy that would extend the learning with chutes and silos, experimented with the materials to determine what the possibilities might be, and then introduced the materials to the toddlers.

OPPORTUNITIES FOR PROBLEM SOLVING WITH CHUTES AND SILOS

Figure 6.7 offers ideas for the kinds of problems very young children might discover and work to solve. It also includes suggestions for educators as they support inquiry learning for the children. Educators will find that similar problem solving occurs within the various activities described in this book.

EDUCATOR PLANNING FOR CHUTES AND SILOS

Materials to Consider for Chutes and Silos Experiences

The thoughtful selection of materials will foster curiosity and creativity, encourage innovation, provide opportunities for language and vocabulary development, enhance development of fine-motor skills, and provide opportunities for social–emotional learning (Geiken, 2011). The tubes from Safe Space Concepts, unlike any others we have found, are easy to clean, are made of a safe material that is shatterproof, and provide for an open-ended experience for infants and toddlers. They are so durable that they have been introduced in museums, where multiple children investigate them on a daily basis.

We do realize that many programs for infants and toddlers have little or no budget for materials. Creative alternatives can provide similar experiences for very young children, such as heavy cardboard tubes from carpet stores, clear plastic flexible tubing from hardware stores, PVC pipe, and so on. Although we prefer transparent tubing, children will still gain experiences from these opaque tubes that allow visualization only through their ends. We have observed the children's interest level remaining high regardless of the kind of tubes offered.

Family members may be willing to provide materials or actively support construction of items shown in photographs in this book. Educators may creatively develop other ideas we have not experienced and that better suit the children in their classrooms.

Additional materials from your own classroom may well be selected when children are encouraged to participate in the gathering of objects that interest them. Be sure to include objects that will not fit into the tubes you have selected. These objects provide opportunities for sorting and classification experiences. Some suggestions are:

- Clear, plastic tubes (sturdy tubes, not flexible) of various diameters (2"–3-1/2") and lengths (12"–36")
- Blocks of various sizes
- Balls of various sizes and materials
- Opaque tubes of various diameters and lengths that can be found at newspaper printers (paper towel or toilet paper tubing is not sturdy enough for this project) or other locations
- Colored scarves
- Materials from the classroom that children bring to the center (block people, bean bags, stuffed animals, loose parts)

Safety of Materials

Educators will want to check the blocks and balls using a choke tube before offering them to the children to be certain that they are safe. If a choke tube is not available, the adult may use a paper towel tube to check the size of the objects that will be used with the tubes.

Infants and toddlers construct knowledge when they produce an action with objects, such as the materials within Chutes and Silos; when the result of their action is immediate and observable; and when there is something for the infant or toddler to vary. Young children will grasp the objects, mouth them, bang them together, toss them, swing the tubes

Age	Problem Solving With Chutes and Silos	How Can Adults Support Children's Problem Solving With Chutes and Silos?
Infant *(0–9 months)*	Grasps tubes, balls, and objects to shake or mouth	Offer child a variety of natural and human-made items to grasp, shake, and mouth
	Acts bored (fusses) when activity and materials are no longer novel	Offer child a variety of natural and human-made items to explore
	Uses hands and eyes together, such as seeing tubes or balls and reaching toward them	Provide safe opportunities for child to reach for toys and explore surroundings
	Chooses from Chutes and Silos materials, rejecting some and exploring others	Provide a variety of balls, tubes, cubes, and scarves for exploration
	Attempts to get tubes and balls when out of reach	Place tubes, balls, and other materials out of reach and encourage child to reach them
	Looks for ball or tube that rolled out of sight	Move materials so they are no longer visible and support child's efforts to look for them
Mobile Infant *(6–12 months)*	Finds tubes, balls, and objects when they are hidden or out of sight	Make a simple game of hiding objects to find
	Imitates actions remembered from previous playtime with tubes and balls	Make comments and ask questions that reflect what the child is doing
	Throws or bounces balls, blows in tubes	Provide materials with common functions, such as cups, balls, scarves, and block people, to use with the tubes
	Imitates adult actions during play with tubes and balls	Model actions with the materials and encourage child to imitate
	Explores tubes and balls and other objects with fingers, hands, and toes	Provide a variety of materials for exploration with the tubes—squishy or squeaky balls, textured blocks, silky scarves
	Demonstrates understanding of cause and effect by rolling balls back and forth, tipping tubes to roll balls, or placing objects inside the tube	Model cause and effect by rolling balls back and forth, tipping tubes to move balls, and putting blocks in and out of the tubes
Toddler *(12–18 months)*	Plays simple games (hiding balls and scarves or hiding behind the screen)	Offer new challenges and problems to solve and join in when child initiates
	Takes turns with adult during play or clean-up with tubes and balls	Support turn-taking by modeling during play or during clean-up
	Works to take tubes apart when they are nested	Gather tubes in a variety of lengths and diameters to encourage stacking, nesting, dumping, and filling
	Explores tubes and materials in a variety of ways—nests, bangs, turns tubes, rolls balls, bats with tubes, dumps and fills	Provide a variety of materials to use with tubes and encourage child to roll, turn, bang, bat, or shake
	Imitates actions of other children or adults in the Chutes and Silos center	Model strategies during play with tubes and encourage child to imitate

(continued)

Figure 6.7. (continued)

Age	Problem Solving With Chutes and Silos	How Can Adults Support Children's Problem Solving With Chutes and Silos?
Toddler (18–24 months)	Plays alongside friend during play	Play near or with children in the Chutes and Silos center in order to anticipate sharing issues and teach age-appropriate conflict resolution
	Uses Chutes and Silos materials in increasingly complex ways such as connecting tubes on the Velcro board with one end higher than the other and putting a ball at the top of the first tube	Observe carefully to determine when the child needs more challenge and provide support when learning new skills
	Points to and names body parts while engaged in Chutes and Silos play	Teach fingerplays or simple songs that teach body parts, or sing "piggyback" songs about what the child is doing ("your pinky's on the tube, your pinky's on the tube, hi-ho the merri-o, your pinky's on the tube")
	Points to and names materials used in Chutes and Silos play	Name the tubes and balls with shape, size, and color words, and encourage child to use those words when talking about their play
Toddler (24–36 months)	Puts balls in one group, scarves in another, tubes together	Provide interesting toys or household objects that can be sorted, nested, and counted, or ask children to select objects from the classroom that they find interesting
	Names or points to materials used with tube and balls play	Make comments and ask questions about the child's work with the materials
	Poses problem (such as fitting balls in tube) and attempts to solve	Provide support by making comments or asking productive questions in order to support problem solving
	Helps to clean up tubes and materials after play	Use clean-up as a way to organize and sort materials
	Recalls and tells others about play with tubes and balls	Ask children questions about what they are doing or narrate what is happening during play. Help to reflect on shared events by initiating a conversation and giving clues when needed.

Note. Adapted from https://sproutsdevelopment.com/resources/problem-solving/

(sometimes swinging to hit the ball or block), and use the tubes to capture balls and blocks.

With these materials, infants and toddlers will have opportunities to compare objects, explore space, use objects as tools, track objects in space, look for missing objects, and construct relationships that build a foundation for later physical science concepts. Some children will think of surprising ways to use the tubes, balls, and blocks. They may stand the tube on end, pack it with the balls and blocks, and then observe what happens when they lift the tube. Some may try to capture balls with one end of the tube or use a tube that is small in diameter to push balls or scarves inside a wide tube. Your questions and comments should reflect what is happening and offer new challenges or problems to solve. Infants and toddlers will have their own questions to investigate and will inspire one another to solve problems. Your children may find new ways to use the materials that we have yet to see. Be open to the possibilities.

CHAPTER 7

Blocks With Infants and Toddlers: Exploring STEM and Problem Solving

Sherri Peterson and Sonia Yoshizawa

TEXTBOX 7.1. CONNOR STACKS BLOCKS

Eighteen-month-old Connor approached the block shelves in his toddler classroom. One of the classroom educators was sitting on the floor nearby observing and interacting with two other toddlers. Connor looked carefully at the materials that were placed there to accompany the mini unit blocks displayed on the shelves, including block people, small vehicles, and a basket of natural wood loose parts. The children in this classroom had been introduced to a variety of blocks in the infant classroom, and educators thought that the toddlers might be intrigued by the large spools, cubes, triangular prisms, wooden pegs, cylinders, cones, and pyramids they had found in a storage room.

Connor began his investigation by pulling the basket of natural wood materials from the shelf and looking them over thoroughly (see Figure 7.1). He lifted each one out of the basket in which they were stored, turned it around in his hand, and then dropped it onto the carpet near his leg. He continued his investigation for several minutes and then began stacking the pieces that he had inspected. He placed a double pillar vertically on the carpet in front of him, and it tipped over. He repositioned it and steadied it with both hands. He picked up one of the large wooden spools and placed it on top of the pillar. He stabilized it, then added a larger spool and a small cylinder, stopping after each addition to position it carefully. He looked up when he was finished and saw his educator observing him. She smiled at him and said, "You stacked four of the wooden shapes. 1, 2, 3, 4. I wonder if there are any more cylinders in your basket?" Connor looked over the shapes and continued stacking until the tower toppled, then began stacking a new tower using the same shapes.

Figure 7.1. Connor Stacks Cylinders

WHY BLOCKS FOR INFANTS AND TODDLERS?

The benefits of block play for young children have been well-documented by both early childhood and STEM experts. Blocks, in particular wooden unit blocks, are one of the best investments an early childhood program can make when selecting classroom materials. These high-quality materials are called "unit blocks" because they are built on the same basic standard of measurement (see Figure 7.2). A unit block is 5.5" long, 2.75" wide, and 1.375" thick. Larger pieces include the double (11" long) and quadruple (22" long) sizes. Smaller sizes are made in various fractions of the standard unit. The mini unit blocks are a smaller version, with the standard unit 11/16" × 1⅜" × 2¾". The blocks that we have found to be most durable are made of maple, a hard wood that does not splinter or crack.

Block play offers opportunities for developing fine- and gross-motor skills, spatial reasoning, hand–eye coordination, problem solving, and foundational math and science concepts, as well as creativity, imagination, and a sense of having solved a self-imposed problem. Infant and toddler educators who include block play as a classroom experience can facilitate the discovery and exploration of blocks, which are the beginning steps of construction and engineering. Block play can be supported for infants and toddlers in developmentally appropriate ways that can provide the foundation for more complex block play for preschool children and beyond (Kamii et al., 2004). As early as 6 months, infants are able to grasp, hold, and examine blocks by shaking and mouthing them. By 12 months, they are beginning to place one block on top of another as they begin to grasp the concept of "on." By 18 months, blocks become a tool for exploring, sorting, balancing, and stacking both vertically and horizontally when toddlers understand "on" and "next to." Two-year-olds begin to recognize that placing blocks carefully will allow them to stack additional blocks to build a tower (Kamii et al., 2004).

Simply having blocks available does not guarantee that block play will provide a high-quality experience for infants and toddlers. Intentional interactions matter. Revisiting block play through the lens of infant and toddler development can assist educators to consider how they can facilitate intellectual growth through their own investigation of the materials, observations of children, thorough documentation, and collaboration with other educators. Young children's engagement in STEM experiences is heightened when adults intentionally plan the environment and the experiences so that children may engage fully with open-ended materials (NSTA, 2014). When educators plan experiences that allow children to explore and investigate by manipulating materials that are carefully chosen for them, it is possible for children to construct mental relationships, develop hypotheses, and organize information. The key to high-quality teaching is to gear activities to children's progressively more complex approaches to understanding the world (Hamlin & Wisneski, 2012).

WHAT DO INFANTS AND TODDLERS DO WITH BLOCKS?

Blocks inspire children to be curious and persistent and to investigate problems and engineer solutions, and can be tailored to individual interests and levels of development. Open-ended materials such as blocks are more likely to provide children with intellectual and emotional satisfaction and support their engagement for extended periods of time than toys with a single purpose (Post et al., 2011). Open-ended materials invite infants and toddlers to engage with the materials as they wonder, use old strategies and develop new ones, develop theories, and find satisfaction with their exploration, the actions taken, and their perceived resolution to self-imposed problems.

Physical Development. Block play is a rich context for physical development as well as language, cognitive, math, science, and social–emotional learning. Infants and toddlers practice eye–hand coordination when they reach for and grasp, knock down, or stack blocks. They develop motor skills as they figure out how to bang, connect, carry, and build with blocks. They encounter the science of physical properties as they reach, grab, drop, chew, smash, and crash a variety of blocks and construct cause-and-effect relationships, develop object permanence, and engage in problem solving.

Language Development. The opportunities for developing spatial language as children play with blocks are abundant. When in the block center with infants, educators may see children respond when

Figure 7.2. Classroom Blocks Shelves for Older Children

asked to "put the blocks in the basket" or "put a big cylinder on top of the tower." Toddlers will begin to understand and use spatial words such as *up*, *on*, *off*, *next to*, *in*, and *out* when investigating blocks. Research has found that the amount of spatial language infants and toddlers are exposed to when engaged with adults is predictive of the amount of spatial language they produce and their performance on spatial tasks (Pruden et al., 2011). The block center offers opportunities to practice new vocabulary as children name materials and describe what they are creating with blocks and the other materials that are gathered to enhance block play. Educators will find many opportunities to model descriptive and spatial language as they observe and participate at the block center.

Cognitive Development. Cognitive skill development is evident as infants and toddlers play with a variety of blocks that are selected for their unique possibilities. When adults participate in block play, they can promote the development of object permanence (the understanding that objects continue to exist even when they cannot be seen, heard, touched, smelled, or sensed). Cause-and-effect relationships are evident when young children watch their educator stack wooden blocks and encourage the babies

to knock them down, or when young toddlers experiment with sounds by knocking blocks together or dropping them into a metal container.

Infants and toddlers engage in mathematics as they notice likenesses and differences, and begin matching, grouping, classifying, and organizing the blocks that are offered. They grapple with spatial thinking as they place blocks on, under, in front of, on top of, and behind one another. When children have the opportunity to engage in block play with support from educators, skills like patterning, symmetry, spatial reasoning, and part–whole relationships will be fostered.

Emotional Development. Finally, through block play, infants and toddlers can exhibit their developing emotional regulation when they show surprise and anticipation as the blocks are introduced, or when they are able to calm themselves when frustrated. Block play provides many opportunities to develop problem-solving skills, the power of imagination, persistence, and confidence in the ability to create.

Developing Skills. In block play, educators will notice a progression that, like inquiry for infants and toddlers, is not linear. Young children will continue to discover more about the properties of the materials as their cognitive and motor skills develop so that they are less dependent on adults to position them or offer them new blocks as they play. Exploration of blocks and the materials offered with them, such as vehicles, loose parts, and materials for dramatic play, will continue long after children are carrying, stacking, and building simple structures. Educators will continue to see children discover new properties or explore with old and new strategies as children become more proficient builders, architects, and engineers.

We offer our ideas about the development of block play for infants and toddlers in order to confirm your understanding about children's development as you begin your own inquiry into what young children do with these materials. We also hope to support you as you plan for new STEM opportunities in your classroom.

There are many resources for educators that list a blocks progression, but these are most often for preschool age or older. In our work we have focused on the actions you typically will see in the infant and toddler years. If you are working with young children who have been identified and qualify for specialized services, you may find that they demonstrate these block behaviors well into the preschool years; in fact, these behaviors may be one indication of delayed development. You also may have children who have had prior experiences that have prepared them to do more advanced building before 36 months. What we do suggest is that no matter the age at which children are introduced to block play, they will discover, explore, carry, and stack before they can become proficient builders. You may observe young children who are discovering and exploring when new materials are introduced, even if they are doing more sophisticated building with familiar blocks. For instance, when older toddlers who have constructed with magnetic blocks are introduced to standard unit blocks, they will require time to learn how to stabilize them by discovering and exploring the unique properties of the wooden blocks.

Forty-month-old Alejandro attended an inclusive early childhood program with 16 children from 34 months to 4 years. He had been served in a home intervention program until shortly before his third birthday, when he was enrolled in the Head Start classroom. The program typically enrolled two or three children with identified special needs, so the educators were adept at removing barriers to learning. The educators' selection of materials and experiences provided a variety of ways for children to access the curriculum; offered multiple means for children to access language and symbols with alternatives for visual and auditory information, such as picture symbols and sign language; and provided children with options for actions and expression when their physical development, language expression and comprehension, or cognitive development required that they have accommodations or modifications (CAST, 2018).

Alejandro could move easily around the room, and his balance in kneeling and walking was continuing to develop. He could use two hands to grab large toys or blocks, hold crayons and markers with his fist in order to make scribbles on paper, and feed himself with a spoon. Alejandro's family spoke Spanish at home, and he was beginning to use a few single words in Spanish with them. When he first joined the classroom, he communicated by shaking his head, smiling when an activity was pleasing to him, or screaming when his needs were not being met. After the first few weeks of school, he began to use simple sign language with prompts to indicate that he needed or wanted something.

His special education educator provided services within the classroom and typically joined Alejandro during center time, where she worked with him alone or in a small group. Alejandro frequently spent time in the blocks and manipulative areas and could sit near another child while playing but was not yet sharing materials. His favorite materials included the magnetic tile blocks (see Figure 7.3), which he easily could manipulate, stack, and combine, or the large plastic interlocking blocks that he could snap together and take apart. He was just beginning to show an interest in the unit blocks, and typically unshelved and piled blocks, and deconstructed structures created by more sophisticated builders. He often watched his friends in the block area, so when his educators met to discuss his individual education plan (IEP), they saw his block activities as addressing cognitive and social–emotional goals.

TEXTBOX 7.2. ALEJANDRO BUILDS A TOWER

On this day, Alejandro and his educator Melanie were seated in the block area. Alejandro selected a large wooden cylinder and placed it on the floor in a vertical position. He selected several more cylinders as well as some large intersection blocks. He stacked those next to the pile of cylinders. He got on his knees, grabbed the cylinders one by one with his right hand, and continued stacking carefully until he had five cylinders in a tower. He paused each time he added a block, looked the tower over warily, then grabbed the next block to add to the tower. After he added the fifth cylinder by reaching up with his arms, he stood, bumped into some building materials that were behind him, stumbled, and then righted himself before he added the sixth block. His educator was kneeling next to the tower observing and documenting his work. She said, "Look at that, Alejandro!" Alejandro looked toward her and touched the top of the tower, which tumbled to the floor. He examined the fallen blocks, moved across the carpet to the block that had been on the top of the tower and sat down. He positioned himself in a sitting position so that he could build with his right hand and began restacking the blocks. His teacher continued to observe and snap photos of his progress while Alejandro rebuilt his tower. Each time he placed a block successfully, he grinned before he grabbed the next one. Several times he bumped the block below the one he was stacking, but he was able to steady the tower by using his left hand to stabilize it. When he placed the fifth block, the tower wobbled a bit but remained in place. Melanie commented, "It stayed. Do you think you can get another one on?" Alejandro looked at her as he grabbed another cylinder and placed it on top. This time the tower wobbled and tumbled down before he could stabilize it and Alejandro began his stacking again.

INFANT TODDLER INQUIRY LEARNING MODEL WITH BLOCKS

In this example we saw Alejandro using familiar strategies with novel materials when he stacked the cylinders that he had selected from the block shelves. His program was rich in materials that were selected carefully by general and special educators for their STEM possibilities. He explored the materials, and we can guess that he made a prediction about the stackability of the large cylinders. He identified the materials and the problem that he

Figure 7.3. Combining Magnetic Blocks With Unit Blocks

wanted to solve, and was persistent in his approach, even after several crashes. He designed and created the tower and solved the stability problem by using his left hand to straighten the blocks after his first tower tumbled. He chose blocks that were the same in order to stack them successfully. The educators wondered whether his planning included thinking about the weight of the cylinders. They were heavier than many of the other blocks and had a solid base on which to build. Alejandro's expressive language development made it difficult to ascertain his planning process, much as with many toddlers.

Alejandro strategized as he continued to investigate the properties of the materials. He began by stacking with his dominant hand only. When the blocks tumbled after the sixth cylinder was added, he began to use his left hand to stabilize the blocks as he stacked. He was persistent as he tried to solve the self-imposed problem of stacking more blocks on the tower before it tumbled, and returned to this activity many times before he was satisfied with the results.

He acknowledged the educator as he stacked and after the blocks tumbled to the floor. We can speculate that he was communicating to Melanie that he wanted her to continue to observe him and photograph his work as he continued with the blocks.

INQUIRY TEACHING MODEL WITH INFANT AND TODDLER BLOCKS

In this example with an older child with identified special needs, we saw educators use their observations of Alejandro to support him with materials that interested him. They predicted that Alejandro would find the unit blocks appealing based on their observation of his interest in what his peers were doing in the block center. They knew that his developing motor skills and his increasing ability to focus on self-selected activities would make blocks and building a robust experience where they could implement the goals and objectives that were part of his IEP.

While Alejandro was in the block center, Melanie continued to observe and to photograph his efforts to stack the cylinders. This allowed her to document his actions for his IEP and for the assessment system that was used for all children in the program. Melanie commented on Alejandro's work briefly, but when she noticed his engagement, she did not bombard him with language. Instead, she saved her comments for specific actions taken, such as when she said, "It stayed. Do you think you can get another one on?" He looked at her several times to see whether she was watching, noticed her photographing him, smiled, and then continued to work. This is what we would call selective intervention. Melanie understood that if she gave Alejandro too much help or offered too many comments, he would be missing out on an opportunity to extend his learning. This is especially important when working with young children who have identified learning needs, who may have few enough opportunities to demonstrate their competence. Here, Alejandro was showing his stuff. He was clearly engaged even when his tower toppled.

Collaboration between the classroom educator and special educator prepared them to support Alejandro as he engaged in building activities. After discussing his interest in building, they determined that they would use picture symbols to help Alejandro communicate when using the materials in the block center. He used some visual supports in the classroom, including a now-next schedule and a choice board for center time. Melanie wanted to add a response board so that Alejandro could indicate wants and needs in a preferred center. They selected a few words that could be used in the block center, such as "More blocks; Blocks crashed; This is fun; I'm ready to go."

Throughout this example, we saw educators making decisions about Alejandro. They communicated frequently to share their observations and found ways to support his learning by adding visual supports in a center where he was ready to communicate his success to the educator. Their actions supported his developing language and encouraged his continued exploration of the blocks as his motor skills and ability to focus on problems increased.

We saw the educators allowing time with the materials so that Alejandro could construct his own knowledge about the properties of the materials and develop confidence in his abilities in his own time and in his own way. This support for young children is essential in an inquiry learning environment and clearly demonstrates the concepts advocated through UDL.

Blocks With Infants

Working with infants with any of the STEM materials we have described requires similar actions from educators. Offering interesting objects and providing support for non-mobile infants so that they can see, hear, feel, smell, and touch them are the main requirements. Later in this chapter we describe a variety of materials and educator actions for engaging with block play (see Figure 7.7).

Many parents and educators believe that infants and toddlers are too young to be able to explore many materials that interest older children. However, we offer vignettes in this chapter that clearly describe young children's interests and experiences with blocks and accessories. As soon as infants can move themselves intentionally, whether their bodies or only their arms and legs, they seek objects to investigate.

TEXTBOX 7.3. WYATT INVESTIGATES UNIT BLOCKS

Six-month-old Wyatt was positioned on the living room floor in front of a basket of toys that included a set of mini unit blocks purchased for him by his grandmother. She had built a structure with a flat foundation, several cylindrical blocks, several units, and some double units that resembled a parking structure. Wyatt was able to roll from front to back and was beginning to scoot around the room on his tummy. When in a prone position he was able to balance on one forearm while reaching for desired objects. When Wyatt noticed the building structure, he pulled himself forward so that he could reach the blocks. He grabbed one of the double units with one hand as the block structure tumbled down. He rolled onto his back and began to investigate the properties of the wooden block by grasping it with one hand, then with both hands, turning it over, touching the flat planes, and grabbing the corners. These mini unit blocks were just the right size and weight for Wyatt to manipulate (see Figure 7.4).

Figure 7.4. Wyatt Explores Blocks

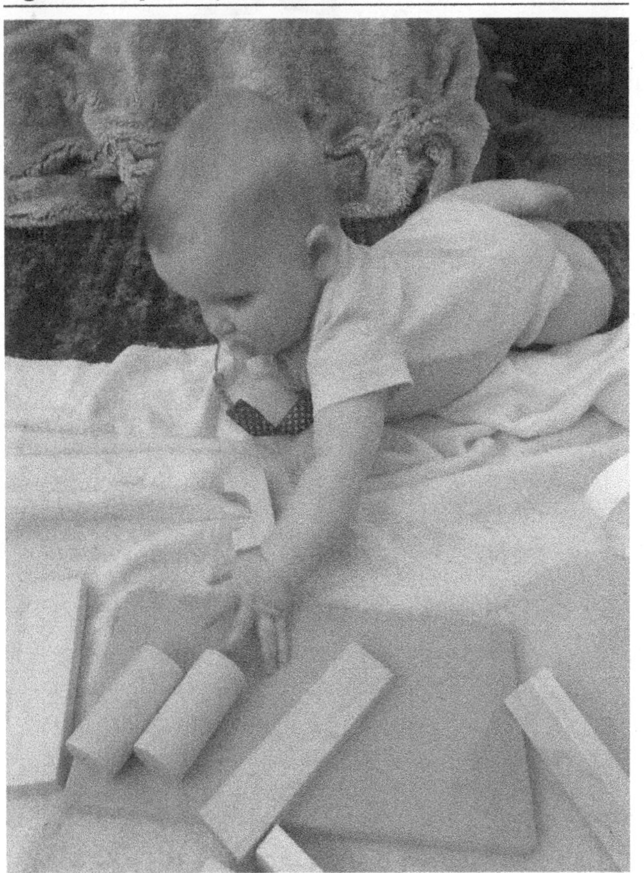

ITM: Engaging Infants. Block play with infants can begin with a small collection of blocks in a variety of shapes, sizes, textures, and sound features that can be handled by the infant. When the educator combines close proximity with descriptive language while engaging with the infant, the experience becomes a powerful interaction. Statements such as, "You dropped the block right next to the tub," or "The block went in the cup and then right back out," surround children with descriptive and spatial language that assists them in making sense of the materials they are exploring. Including some textured or soft, squishy blocks provides interest and encourages differentiation. Blocks with bells or lights engage children with other sensory modalities and may be more engaging for infants with sensory deficits. Educators can respond with a simple acknowledgment when the infant shakes a block with a bell or rattle, or tracks a block that is held at eye level. Infants will be engaged easily with just a few interesting blocks that capitalize on their natural curiosity.

Educators can demonstrate how to use blocks in different ways and invite participation by positioning non-mobile infants so that they can reach and grasp the blocks. In the example with Wyatt, the block structure was placed slightly out of reach so that he was enticed to move toward it. It provided a target that rewarded him with a crash when he reached toward and grabbed a block. The size of the mini unit blocks allowed Wyatt to easily manipulate them to discover their physical properties and to practice more refined movements as he grasped a block.

ITM: Providing Opportunities. Educators can provide opportunities for infants by selecting blocks that have properties that will encourage discovery and exploration. Soft, squeezable blocks, textured cloth blocks, mini unit blocks, bristle blocks, or nesting blocks offer infants possibilities to encounter sensory experiences that are novel and interesting. Infants do not need a large quantity of blocks, but it is important that there be enough variety so that interest can be stimulated with all of the infants. Educators can document children engaged in problem solving when an infant scoots forward to knock over a stack of large cloth blocks, or in developing object permanence when an infant searches for a block that is hidden under a basket or behind the shelves. Infants develop understanding about the unique properties of blocks when they encounter blocks that can be grasped, released, mouthed, and crashed. Educators can provide opportunities for building vocabulary as they narrate the actions of the child or use self-talk to describe their own actions as they join the play.

ITM: Making Decisions. Educators who work with infants make decisions about the most effective way to provide support when children are engaging with blocks. The relationship between the adult and child and the knowledge that the educator has about the learning dispositions of each child give educators insight into this selective intervention. In the example with Wyatt, his grandmother knew that he was able to engage in solitary play with materials that interested him for ever-increasing periods of time and that he would attempt to solve self-imposed problems without adult mediation. If an adult intervened too quickly, he would lose interest and move away from the activity or begin to fuss. She continued to observe him with the block until he had completed his exploration, and then designed another structure just out of reach so that she could determine whether his interest would continue. When her observations suggested that he was no longer interested, she made the decision to move a basket of large interlocking blocks toward him for exploration. As she introduced these new materials, she labeled the blocks and used spatial language to describe their location: "Look at the blocks in this basket, Wyatt. They are lighter than the wooden blocks and have bright colors. Oh, you put the red one in your right hand and then grabbed it with your left hand. Now you dropped the green block right beside the blue one."

Blocks With Young Toddlers

In the example with Jake (see Figure 7.5 and Textbox 7.4), we clearly can see the ITILM at work. He spent some time in the wonder stage as he investigated the mega blocks by turning them over and inspecting their unique properties. We can only guess at his thinking, but he appeared to understand that the pegs on the bottom of the blocks were significant. He used some familiar strategies to remove more blocks from the basket and placed them in piles around his body.

When he selected a block and a small stack that was already connected and said, "Here," we wondered whether he had made sense of the way the

Figure 7.5. Jake Builds With Plastic Blocks

blocks could be put together. He then connected the single block to the stack and squealed with delight, which seemed to signal that his goal had been met. He then posed another problem for himself as he disconnected the block. Jake continued to practice and observed how the materials and actions worked.

TEXTBOX 7.4. CONNECTING BLOCKS

Seventeen-month-old Jake sat amid a pile of mega blocks on the classroom floor. His educator sat nearby observing Jake as he investigated the blocks. Jake dropped several of the smaller mega blocks on his lap and then picked up a larger block and turned it over to look at the underside. He then selected a small stack of blocks, held it with both hands as he looked at the place where they were connected, then dropped the stack on the other side of his lap, and said "Here."

Jake picked up one of the smallest blocks and connected it to the stack beside him with his right hand, then repeated this action with another block. He squealed with delight, picked up the stack, and removed the blocks he had just connected. He looked his selection of blocks over carefully and added a larger block in the place where he had just removed the block. He continued to add blocks to the tower, holding the stack with his left hand while placing blocks with his right hand. He stopped, placed the stack on his lap again, removed the block on top, and carefully observed the pegs on top as he held the block in both hands.

Jake attempted to reconnect the block to the stack. He did not appear to be aware that some of the blocks were now disconnected and added a small block to the top. He picked up the bottom segment and added an identical block to the stack. He selected the top section from the floor and tried to add a block. When it did not connect easily, he lifted it higher to look at it and noticed that the block on top was a smaller size than the block he was attempting to connect. He dropped that block, removed the smaller block from the top of the stack, and added the block that matched the others. When Jake had connected it to make a tower of four same-sized blocks, he began to disconnect them and drop them on the floor.

When he encountered a problem as he tried to attach the small block to a stack of longer blocks, he looked it over carefully. It appeared that he noticed the difference in size and decided that was the problem. Jake then found a block that matched so that he could connect it more easily. Although he resolved this problem, he continued to connect and disconnect the blocks as if to verify his theory.

ITM: *Engaging Young Toddlers.* Young toddlers will embrace the block center as educators add new materials that are designed for open-ended play and fine-motor challenges. Jake had the opportunity to explore blocks in both the infant and toddler classrooms and had engaged in other STEM experiences. His educators knew that with his developing motor and cognitive skills, he would find the mega blocks a challenge. In this example, he clearly was engaged in figuring out how the blocks connected. The educator who was nearby did not interrupt his investigation as he connected and disconnected the blocks, carefully inspected their unique properties, and developed new strategies that would help him solve the problem he had posed for himself. Jake's engagement in this experience extended for several play periods as he compared the blocks and considered the pieces that he needed in order to complete a project.

ITM: *Providing Opportunities.* In this example with Jake, the educator who was observing him recognized that her role was as an observer and documenter of the learning taking place. Jake was fully engaged in his work, and any kind of communication or attempts to support or validate Jake's work might have derailed his investigation. Sometimes this is the hardest thing for educators to do. Our training suggests that our role is to "teach" young children or to praise them when they have success. With infants and toddlers, our most important contribution to their learning is simply to set up a safe and engaging environment, develop trusting relationships with the children, and invite them to investigate the materials. In Jake's classroom, these things were in place, and he was in charge of his learning about the mega blocks. His educator's role was to observe and record so that she could make decisions about how to continue to challenge Jake.

ITM: *Making Decisions.* Jake's educator learned much from this observation that could be used to further expand his abilities. She might introduce smaller blocks that could be connected or provide some models for him to replicate. His developing fine-motor coordination might suggest that he was ready to assemble non-interlocking puzzles or complete more of his dressing routine when preparing for outdoor play. She also might challenge him with the same materials by intervening with some comments or questions that suggested additional moves he could make with the blocks. In this example, the educator recognized that her intervention was not required. Jake was fully engaged with an experience that challenged him at just the right level.

Blocks With Older Toddlers

Amira entered the classroom with an enthusiastic greeting to educators, hugged her daddy, and sent him on his way so that she could get to work. She had been at the child care center since infancy and had many opportunities to engage in STEM centers. She had played with a variety of blocks, including mini unit blocks, and was a confident builder.

The educators had gathered a bin of wooden "block leftovers" from the storage area. The blocks

Figure 7.6. Amira Examines Blocks

included some three-dimensional wooden shapes, cubes, rectangular prisms, and wooden craft pieces, along with circus animals, a circus wagon, and a ringmaster (see Figure 7.6).

Amira was actively engaged in the inquiry learning process as she constructed her towers. It was evident that she had prior experiences with building materials. She selectively chose particular blocks for her towers. When she encountered a problem with stability, she rearranged the tower by removing blocks and placing the cone on top of the short, wide cylinder. With inquiry, we find that the more familiar children become with the materials, the more strategies they can employ to solve the problems they have posed for themselves.

Textbox 7.5. Amira Is a Skilled Builder

Thirty-month-old Amira joined two friends at a small table in her toddler classroom. Each had a small pile of wooden block pieces. Amira bent over the container holding the materials and began to select individual wooden shapes. She carefully inspected several of the larger blocks as she lifted them out onto the table. She began by selecting the longest block and placing it in an upright position. She looked at the block choices, selected a cube, and placed that on top of the taller block. She then carefully stacked a long block in a horizontal position, then a short, wide cylinder, and finally two longer cylinders one on top of the other. She then looked into the tub again and selected a large wooden cone. When the cone was added, it toppled along with the two skinny cylinders. She picked up the cone and inspected the bottom of it and looked at the remaining blocks in the tower. She added the cone to the top of the wide cylinder and stepped back to look at it. The bottom of the cone and the top of the cylinder were the same size, so the tower was more stable than the first tower she built. She continued to investigate the blocks and began to build another tower. The first three blocks she stacked were thin rectangular prisms, and these were stacked horizontally on the table. She then added three pillars that she placed vertically on top of one another. She used two hands to stabilize the pillars before she added a short cylinder, and another pillar that was possible only when she stood on her tiptoes. The tower was now so tall that she could no longer reach to add more blocks. One of the other toddlers was sitting near her at the table as she worked. When she had completed the second tower, he said, "Whoa." She looked over at him and smiled her acceptance of his interest. Amira noticed the circus animals and props. She began to arrange them near her towers and move them around on the table.

Amira's problem of building a stable tower was solved when she used her prior knowledge about building to find a way to stack the blocks she had selected. We also saw that she was not satisfied after building the first tower and continued to challenge herself to create something new. She repeated her successful strategy when using different materials until she was satisfied with her result. When she had completed her work (or resolved her self-imposed problem), she examined the new materials and used them to engage in dramatic play with the blocks. We expect that she will continue to use her new strategies as she engages with other kinds of building materials.

*ITM: **Engaging Older Toddlers.*** In this example we see an older toddler who has had some experience with blocks approach the table with her customary enthusiasm for new materials and challenge herself to build a tower. The educators in this classroom had identified the interests of the children from their daily observations and made a decision to add some interesting new materials to the block area. They wanted to engage all the children in building experiences and decided that with the addition of these wooden blocks with interesting properties and some appealing props, they might see an explosion of interest. For Amira, the blocks were the initial enticement, but when she was ready to move to a new activity, the props elevated the experience for her.

*ITM: **Providing Opportunities.*** The educators in Amira's room provided a STEM experience where children could produce a result (a tower) that was immediate (the tower either stood or toppled), was observable (they could see that it fell down or stayed up), and allowed for variables (Amira could change the blocks for a different result). In our view, that is a high-quality STEM experience that invites inquiry. Amira was engaged in the experience, and the learning that was taking place as she adjusted her tower to make it more stable was identifiable. There were other materials available to her when she was ready to try something new, and her educators supported her decisions about what she wanted to do. They supported her by observing and documenting, and with their proximity if she needed them.

*ITM: **Making Decisions.*** Educators of infants and toddlers make decisions throughout their day. Many of these decisions involve the intentional selection of materials that will engage all the children in the classroom. In this example with Amira, the educators planned an environment that allowed the children to choose from an array of interesting materials that could provide opportunities for engaging their developing motor, cognitive, language, and social–emotional skills. Their support took shape as they observed children's actions and determined how to support each child in the experiences they selected. These observations provided documentation for assessment and gave insight into children's interests for future planning.

EDUCATOR PLANNING FOR BLOCKS

Young Children's Actions With Blocks

We caution you about the terms typically used when describing what young children do with blocks. The words *progressions*, *stages*, or *trajectories* may imply to educators or parents that children move through block play in a linear fashion. In our work with infants and toddlers, we see children engage in discovery and exploration throughout the early years as new materials are offered to them. Your observations and documentation will help you to determine what actions children are demonstrating as they use these appealing materials.

Figure 7.7 describes the actions you may observe when infants and toddlers engage with blocks. The table also includes which children's ideas educators can support as they observe, as well as suggestions for questions or comments they might use. As children gain experience, educators also may suggest challenges to support children's actions. The information in this table is a combination of other researchers' ideas about how preschoolers and older children engage with blocks (Chalufour & Worth, 2004; Clements & Sarama, 2009; Johnson, 1933/1996), along with our own experiences with younger children.

In our work with older toddlers, we have not observed children under 3 engaged in bridging; however, you may observe this kind of block play in your program if you have children who have had prior experiences with building activities. We caution you to observe as building expertise unfolds rather than trying to teach a building skill that a toddler is not yet ready to do. This can lead to children losing interest in the block center or losing confidence in themselves as builders.

Preparing for Block Play

When introducing blocks to infants and very young toddlers, educators may choose to place blocks in attractive baskets, colorful plastic bins, or stacked on low shelves (see Figure 7.8). Labeling the containers with photographs is a way to keep the blocks organized and assist children and adults in clean-up.

Once children are beginning to carry, stack, or build more sophisticated structures, it is important

Figure 7.7. Young Children's Actions With Blocks

Child Behavior	Ideas to Support	Questions/Comments/Challenges
Stage 1: Discovering Investigates materials to learn about the properties of blocks by gazing, touching, grasping, holding, mouthing Tracks brightly colored blocks or blocks with a sound feature from side to side Swipes and knocks down a small stack of blocks	Provide blocks in a variety of colors, patterns, sizes, textures, and shapes Organize the blocks so that children can see the similarities and differences when they begin to select blocks independently Offer blocks with a sound feature, such as a soft block with a bell inside Demonstrate different ways to play with blocks—stacking, tapping, grasping, feeling Place interesting blocks just out of reach so infants are encouraged to move Build a tower and place it near the infant's feet so they can kick it down Place blocks in front of or on top of a mirror	Use descriptive language to label blocks as infants begin to construct physical knowledge Use spatial language to describe the location of the blocks Use engaging responses when the infant handles the blocks Entice infants to engage in sensory motor play by sitting nearby, stacking and unstacking, filling and emptying containers
Stage 2: Exploring Continues to investigate materials with old and new strategies Observes the results of actions taken and tries again with the same or different strategies Drops blocks into containers or dumps them into piles Hits or taps blocks together or against other objects Knocks down small towers Plays with blocks independently for short periods of time	Arrange blocks so that children can easily see their attributes Provide a variety of baskets, boxes, and tubs to fill with blocks Build towers for infants to knock down Place a block under a cloth and observe to see whether the infant demonstrates object permanence—the block is still there! Demonstrate stacking, dumping, piling, containing, and combining blocks in different ways	Use descriptive language to label blocks—you fit the red blocks together; there are two cylinders in your basket Use spatial language to describe the location of the blocks—you put three unit blocks in the basket; you stacked the blocks with two cubes on top of the big unit block Use engaging responses when the infant uses the blocks—laugh or squeal with delight Make up silly "piggyback" songs about the actions the child is taking with blocks—little Caleb dumped the blocks, BOOM-O, BOOM-O, CRASH (to the tune of *Old MacDonald*) Observe for signs that the infant is ready for a play partner—looking at the adult, reaching out to share
Stage 3: Carrying Carries blocks from one part of the classroom or playground to another Is able to notice similarities and differences when handling the blocks Begins to match the shapes of the blocks	Add more blocks to the area and arrange them so children easily can select blocks with specific attributes Provide wagons for hauling blocks from one part of the room or playground to another Provide buckets or baskets so that toddlers can carry a quantity of blocks Offer boxes that can be filled with blocks Find some small suitcases, purses, or briefcases to pack with blocks Rotate kinds of blocks regularly to provide a range of block sizes, shapes, and types	You have a lot of blocks in a line. What else could you do with those blocks? I wonder whether these blocks will fit in this box. You figured out how to get all of the blocks into the box. You filled the wagon with blocks. I wonder whether it will be hard to pull. Some of the blocks are the same and some are different. I wonder whether you could find all of the blocks that look like this one.

Child Behavior	Ideas to Support	Questions/Comments/Challenges
Stage 4: Stacking Stacks blocks either vertically (towers) or horizontally (rows) May not be selective about what blocks to stack at first, but later understands that stacking similar blocks works better Begins to build sets of rows and towers Rows may begin to go in different directions, making corners Begins to be meticulous (demonstrating toddler is noticing congruence) Demonstrates flexibility in integrating parts of the structure	Offer cars, trucks, and other vehicles and road signs to encourage building Add small creatures or people for pretend play with the blocks Provide floor mats, place mats, or flat wooden pieces to make structures with more stability Provide a light table or pad with translucent, transparent, and opaque building materials Display blocks so that there is easy access, ample space for play, and children can participate in clean-up Post pictures of interesting construction or make a book with laminated photos of buildings and natural phenomena; or post a book of children's constructions	I see you are putting the blocks on top of each other. Should we find more blocks that would work? You stacked all of the blocks and then they fell down. Is there another way that you could do that? You used the same blocks to make your road. Should we find some blocks that are different? I notice you are laying the blocks next to each other. You made a house for your family. The mommy is standing near the baby. You made a long road. Let's count how many blocks you used. One, two, three . . . It looks like your tower is higher than your friend's tower. Let's see whether you used more blocks or different blocks. You stacked these blocks the tall way. I wonder if there is another way you could stack them so the tower will stay standing? You have a long row and a short row. Can you show me how you did that? It looks like you used four squares in this one and four rectangles in that one. Are they the same? I see you used a long double unit on the bottom, and then you put two unit blocks on top to match. They fit just perfectly. You put the triangle at the very top of the rectangles! Look here! That is a corner where you changed the direction of the blocks.
Stage 5: Bridging Bridges the space between two upright blocks with a third block Often makes enclosures at the same time as bridges Often begins by holding top piece and placing ends beneath	Model bridging when playing with children Display pictures of bridges or columns	You made the top block balance. I bet that wasn't easy. Some of your blocks lie down and some stand up. You could drive a car through this space! Have you tried any other kinds of blocks? How did that work? You have some windows in your structure! I can look through them at you! Last week you were building structures with one level. Now you have three!

Figure 7.8. Block Shelves for Infants

that unit blocks are sorted and neatly arranged. Intentional educators categorize them so that children easily can view the variety of blocks that are available. Placing them with the long side in view enables children to see the size of each type of block. When blocks are dumped in a bin or tub, children will have difficulty finding the needed sizes. They simply will scatter blocks unnecessarily if you store them in a bin or place them randomly on the shelves. Placing block-shaped cutouts covered with clear tape or contact paper on the shelves will assist children at clean-up time. Until they become mobile, infants will be able to participate in the clean-up by dropping blocks into bins or baskets so that adults can place them on the block shelves.

Educators can assist toddlers to name and categorize blocks during clean-up by giving very specific directions that include descriptors such as "find all of the blocks that look like this one," or "the hollow blocks go right here on the bottom because they are very heavy," or "these blocks are longer than those blocks, so let's find all of the short ones for this shelf." Educators who remember that clean-up in the block center is a math experience realize that this activity is equally as important as building.

Block accessories can be added based on the interests of children or a particular event that occurs in the center. For instance, children in one center we are familiar with placed construction vehicles in the block center after a walk that took them to a neighborhood where construction was in progress. The educators took photos of some of the action and added these to the block center. The children were inspired to haul blocks from one end of the room to the other in their trucks. With support from the educators, they were able to begin stacking blocks and making roads for the trucks with the large blocks. Adults will want to avoid setting out so much that children have difficulty selecting materials or the floor becomes littered with so many building materials that there is no longer room to carry, build, and knock down their structures. Observing carefully what children are using and doing allows educators to remove materials that are no longer of interest to the children. Listening carefully to their words helps determine additional interests.

Strategies for Adding Blocks to Your Classroom

Offering materials that stimulate all the senses is an essential task for educators of infants and toddlers.

Providing a wide variety of blocks for the classroom can ensure that interest is awakened in every child.

Wooden unit blocks and mini unit blocks are a big investment for an infant and toddler program, but one we think is well worth the expense. High-quality maple unit blocks last for many years; in fact, we have seen blocks in classrooms that were more than 50 years old. In one program where we worked with educators, some of their highly valued unit blocks were found in a maintenance room. We urge you to investigate the spaces in your own center or nearby elementary schools to determine whether there are any materials stored in unlikely places. We also have found affordably priced unit blocks and loose parts at tag sales and resale shops. Asking parents or parent groups for their assistance in procuring these important materials is another way to add blocks to your program.

In one community where we have worked, there are mini grants for which educators can apply, and local businesses that support education with time and materials. You can ask construction, engineering, or architectural firms in your community for assistance in procuring building materials. The professionals in these fields will understand the importance of providing opportunities for children to construct and engineer with high-quality materials. Partnerships with high school or community college industrial technology programs may provide a means for procuring blocks for your children's program, with special care taken to ensure that the block preparation provides safe materials that will not splinter. Some school districts have Partners in Education who support schools with time and resources and could be a resource for assisting schools with obtaining the funding for blocks. Wooden unit blocks are essential for making the most of block play.

Building with blocks provides an opportunity for developmental growth in several important domains of learning. Your role as an educator is to carefully select high-quality building materials, provide time and ample space for building, and trust young children as they choose experiences that interest them (see Figure 7.9). Our experiences with infant and toddler block play are in the initial phases of understanding. We urge you to contemplate what we have observed and continue learning about what children do with blocks and building materials in your own program.

Figure 7.9. Blocks for Toddlers

CHAPTER 8

Light and Shadow Experiences With Infants and Toddlers

Exploring Spatial Understanding and Problem Solving

Sherri Peterson and Jill Uhlenberg

> **TEXTBOX 8.1. AYSHA SOLVES A PROBLEM**
>
> Aysha (30 months) came to the Light and Shadow center set up in a darkened corner of the classroom and watched as her friends explored the materials that were available to them. Tiffany, one of the educators in the classroom, sat near the overhead projector (OHP) as the children were taking turns trying out the materials on the bed of the OHP and observing the results on the large canvas screen set up a few feet away. Aysha watched as several children worked and then moved near the screen to look at the display. She touched the screen, turned to the OHP, and then looked at the screen and touched it. When it was her turn, she selected from an assortment of laminated materials (string, yarn, paper with holes, tissue paper designs) that were placed near the OHP. She placed two of the laminated items on top of the bulb that sits above the bed of the projector and turned toward the screen as she held the sheets in place (see Figure 8.1). When she noticed that there was no change on the screen, she turned back to the OHP and tried another overlay. She repeated this action several times as Tiffany observed her efforts. Tiffany commented, "I wonder if there is another place you could put those?" Aysha continued to place the overlays on the OHP bulb, looked at the results, and then tried again. Tiffany pointed to the bed of the OHP. Aysha ignored her prompt and continued her investigation by placing the overlay on the bulb. After several more attempts with this placement, she laid material down on the bed of the OHP. Tiffany and a student worker erupted into excited squeals and pointed to the screen. Aysha turned around to see what all the excitement was about. She exchanged grins with Tiffany.

WHY LIGHT AND SHADOW WITH INFANTS AND TODDLERS?

Young children are captivated by light and shadows (see Figure 8.2). How often have you watched as a young child notices a shadow move or change? Have you found yourself taking a photo of an interesting shadow and sharing it with friends on social media? In our work with educators, we have observed that when they are presented with an opportunity to investigate light and shadows, they are as intrigued as their children. Young children and their educators share this fascination with an interesting phenomenon that is a limitless resource for creating an engaging STEM experience. "From birth children confront light and shadows. Like holes, shadows exist only because of concrete objects. They are confusing because they represent a paradox—existence and non-existence" (Lewin-Benham, 2010, p. 145). We have explored this STEM interest area with educators in infant and toddler environments as well as with those who work with children from preschool to 3rd grade. We gain insight into children's self-confidence, competencies, and prior experiences when they are provided with interesting materials, the time to explore them, and the support

Figure 8.1. Aysha Examines Her Shadow on the Large Screen

of educators who have investigated the materials themselves before introducing light and shadows to children.

Experiences that are selected for study with young children must be

- drawn from the environment in which they live,
- concepts that are important to science,
- interesting and engaging to both adults and children, and
- phenomena that can be explored in depth over time (Worth, 2010).

INFANT TODDLER INQUIRY LEARNING MODEL WITH LIGHT AND SHADOW

For infants and young toddlers, the main focus of the explorations of Light and Shadow will be light. As children become more experienced and more mobile, their interest will expand to include finding and making shadows.

In this example with Aysha and her educators, we see evidence of her wonder as she investigated the materials that were provided for the toddlers in her classroom. The newly added materials in the

Figure 8.2. Exploring Shadows Outside

classroom engaged her in wondering about the physical characteristics of the laminated overlays to make sense of them. She went to the screen and used her hands to touch the images being displayed when a friend was at the overhead projector. Aysha eagerly approached the OHP when her friend had completed a turn, adding materials to the bulb of the OHP.

Aysha's Persistence

Aysha continued to examine the materials, then chose an overlay, placed it on the bulb, and looked at the screen. She could see that the screen was blank and picked up a different overlay, placed it on the bulb, and looked at the screen again. She repeatedly used this strategy to try to create a display on the screen. Her attempts to produce a display on the screen using the strategy of placing the overlay on the bulb of the OHP did not produce the results she expected. Aysha's prior experiences with Light and Shadow materials such as LED lights and portable light tables may have suggested to her that the materials go on the bulb.

It is notable that even when young children watch others use new materials or strategies to get interesting results, they continue to try out their ideas until they are convinced that the strategy is not working. Often, even scaffolding from an adult does not change the child's thinking about how to make something interesting happen! (Remember that *wet paint* sign?) When educators capitalize on the natural curiosity of children and identify their prior knowledge, educators can facilitate exploration and support problem solving. Documenting what children know and can do allows for decision-making based on children's interests, learning preferences, and individual goals.

Tiffany gave Aysha several hints about what she could try with the materials, but Aysha continued to place the overlays on the bulb. After trying this strategy for several minutes, she set one of the overlays on the bed of the projector. When the educator responded with excited feedback, Aysha looked at Tiffany and then at the display on the screen with interest and wonder. She continued to use the materials on the bed of the OHP with her new strategy. The educators considered that Aysha had accepted this solution and that the problem she had posed for herself had been resolved.

When the OHP and the overlay materials were available on the following day, Aysha came to the Light and Shadow center with a friend and indicated her interest in continuing her investigation of the OHP. She looked over the selection that was offered for investigation, selected an overlay, and placed it on the bulb! We wondered about her use of the same strategy that had been used during her initial investigation of the materials. Because we understand how important extended time with the materials is for inquiry learning, we considered that Aysha required more time with the materials and the phenomena to fully understand the relationship between the placement of the materials and the image on the screen.

Overlapping Wave Theory

Our first observation suggested that Aysha understood this relationship because she repeated her new strategy several times after the educator reacted to what was deemed success. When she returned to the center the next day and repeated the first strategy, we considered that she had not accepted this solution to the identified problem. It appeared that Aysha automatically reverted to the old strategy.

Very young children often revert to previously used strategies when they encounter new materials or new situations. This returning to known and comfortable strategies demonstrates the "overlapping wave theory" of young children's problem solving (Chen et al., 2000). For instance, Aysha previously had used the artist light pads where she placed materials on that lighted surface. This strategy allowed her to consider the properties of the materials. With the OHP, she again placed materials on the light source, but this time the results were different. She needed more time to observe how the materials and her actions worked or did not work. If she remained persistent, she would move to new and different strategies to find success.

We further considered what the reaction of the educator had communicated. Did Aysha continue with the new strategy because of the response she received when she placed the overlays on the bed of the projector? That possibility became apparent the next time Aysha used the OHP with the old unsuccessful strategies. Even though the educators assumed she had figured out how to be successful with the OHP, Aysha reverted to her previous approach. She needed to make her own discoveries about how the OHP and materials worked—a clear example of inquiry learning.

INQUIRY TEACHING MODEL WITH LIGHT AND SHADOW

The educators in Aysha's classroom supported inquiry learning by providing opportunities to engage learners with appealing materials that provided the possibility to activate prior knowledge and experiences. The program had a large freestanding light table that was shared by all of the infant and toddler classrooms. The educators in the program had observed and documented the children's interest and investigation of the materials provided at the light table. During their collaborative work time, they brainstormed ideas for adding to their investigation of light and shadows.

An overhead projector and a large screen made with plastic pipes and a shower curtain were acquired, and educators inventoried their classroom materials to find items that could provide interest and challenges at the OHP. They planned several other centers that were of high interest to avoid bunching up at the Light and Shadow center. The OHP and the large screen were placed in an area of the room that could be darkened easily, and centers that required more light were placed close to the natural light sources so that overhead lights could be turned off.

The educator observed Aysha as she approached the Light and Shadow center and waited for her turn. She saw Aysha look over the laminated overlays and then move toward the screen to contemplate the display. She considered that this lengthy observation of other children's exploration indicated that Aysha had a clear understanding of the relationship between the OHP and the screen.

When it was Aysha's turn to use the OHP, she placed the overlay on the bulb, looked from the materials to the screen, and repeated this move several times. Tiffany supported her problem solving by giving her time to accomplish the goal she set for herself. Aysha looked over at the educator several times to communicate her awareness of Tiffany's interest in her work. Tiffany provided some cues such as, "Is there another place you could put that?" After

several rounds of selecting new overlays and positioning each on the bulb, Aysha placed one of the overlays on the bed of the OHP. Tiffany and the other adult immediately saw that Aysha had produced a display on the screen and called her attention to it. She communicated her delight with a big grin and repeated her action several times.

When Aysha returned to the OHP on the following day and continued her old strategy of placing the overlay on the bulb, Tiffany reflected on her previous observations and documentation of Aysha's learning. As she thought about her reaction following Aysha's initial success, she considered whether these actions supported or impeded Aysha's problem solving. She contemplated her assumption that Aysha had solved her problem, and how to respond in better ways to children's actions. She continued to facilitate Aysha's exploration of the OHP and materials as she checked for Aysha's understanding of the phenomena and supported her further problem solving, noting her persistence in experimenting with the OHP.

Video, photographs, and notes taken during Aysha's Light and Shadow investigations, as well as educators' reflections on her experiences in other STEM learning centers, supported their planning for new explorations. Their insights into how the children strategized and modified their actions became more important to their planning.

Light and Shadow Experiences With Infants

Maria had planned the environment and added interesting materials to provide a context for learning in the infant room rather than a specific lesson with educator goals and expectations (Lally, 2009). She wanted to offer experiences with lights and had prepared a tub of various light sources, including small flashlights and clear plastic bottles with fairy lights placed inside to use with the infants. While the more mobile infants explored, Maria focused her time on Ava, a 4-month-old child.

TEXTBOX 8.2. AVA ADMIRES FAIRY LIGHTS

Ava sat in her bouncy seat near the mobile infants and her educator, Maria. The lights had been dimmed and Maria noticed that Ava was alert and active, so she selected a small clear mailing tube filled with fairy lights. She moved closer to Ava. Maria shifted the tube from left to right across Ava's field of vision. Ava followed the tube visually as Maria moved it back and forth while labeling the materials and describing her actions (see Figure 8.3). Ava continued to track the tube as Maria moved it. She began to kick her feet and wave her arms up and down as she gazed at the twinkling lights. She looked toward Maria and smiled as she continued to move her body enthusiastically.

Maria observed Ava's alert state, which was inferred as wonder about the actions of the mobile infants. She made a decision to stimulate Ava's interest by capitalizing on Ava's natural curiosity about the world around her. Maria's knowledge about Ava's prior experiences with Light and Shadow materials, and her awareness of the importance of providing non-mobile infants with novel experiences, paired

Figure 8.3. Ava Tracks the Fairy Light Container

with back-and-forth exchanges when they are alert and awake, made this a powerful interaction. Her observation and documentation during the exchange assisted her in providing additional experiences for the youngest learners in the classroom.

ITM: Engaging Infants. In infant classrooms, Light and Shadow experiences may begin with a variety of transparent and translucent containers filled with human-made light sources such as fairy lights, colored tea lights, and closet push-lights. Educators may think about prior STEM experiences that infants have had, and can plan to capitalize on their natural curiosity as they select materials and space for this investigation. Light sources can be placed on a table in a corner of the darkened classroom or on low shelves that are easy for mobile infants to access. Adults who are closest to the children can observe their interest in the light sources and add materials as needed.

As educators observe, they may be guided by questions such as these:

- How can we introduce Light and Shadow materials safely to infants?
- Where can we place the human-made light sources so the infants can access them?
- What happens when we alter the natural light in the classroom?
- What do we observe about how the youngest infants respond to the array of natural and human-made light sources?
- What is the most effective way for educators to stimulate interest in the human-made light sources for infants who are not yet mobile?
- How can we activate prior knowledge and experience with Light and Shadow materials?
- What are some specific actions we saw the infants use with the materials?
- How can we document our observations about what they notice and wonder about?

Planning for next steps may focus on these questions and on formal discussions with other educators in the classroom after each experience. In one classroom, an observation of infant explorations and photos viewed on an educator blog post prompted educators to find a place where the infants could crawl inside an enclosure so that the lights could be adjusted more effectively than those in the classroom. The educators emptied a large, low cupboard, removed the doors, and added a curtain so that the light could be adjusted inside this "hidey-hole."

The infants enjoyed this new space and crawled in and out repeatedly. They pushed the curtain aside and watched for the educators to engage with them in a game of peek-a-boo. After exploring the space, the infants focused on the push-lights mounted on the side of the cupboard.

> **TEXTBOX 8.3. CARLY EXPLORES THE PUSH-LIGHT**
>
> Carly moved the curtain in the hidey-hole and gazed at a closet push-light attached to the wall inside the space. When she was able to remove it from the Velcro attachment, she examined it by tilting, turning, shaking, and then mouthing it (see Figure 8.4).

Educators may observe that when plastic containers filled with tea lights or twinkle lights are introduced, the infants explore the containers with the same strategies that are observed when they explore containers such as plastic storage boxes, baskets, buckets, and bags. They may reach for them, shake or pound them, and transport them. They may use their hands and mouth to explore them in order to understand the properties of the objects and what the possibilities are for investigating them. They may attend to the lights inside the containers for brief periods but then return to their tried-and-true routines. Infants will need many opportunities over time to discover new strategies and to attend to the added property of light.

A portable light table that can be moved easily to different places in the classroom can be another provocation for infants who can move. Educators can gather a variety of materials to be placed near the light table on a low surface. Placing the table next to a wall with an outlet can help to keep the cords out of sight so that infants can focus on the light table and the objects.

Mobile infants will require monitoring, and items to be explored will need to be examined for safety for the experience to be suitable for infants. Additional materials that can be introduced to infants include a "moon ball" that changes colors as the children touch and move it, child-friendly flashlights, wall washers, disco lights, and a screen paired with an LED light.

An overhead projector will delight older infants and will offer interest for long periods of time.

Figure 8.4. Carly Tastes a Push-Light

Figure 8.5. Exploring the Overhead Projector

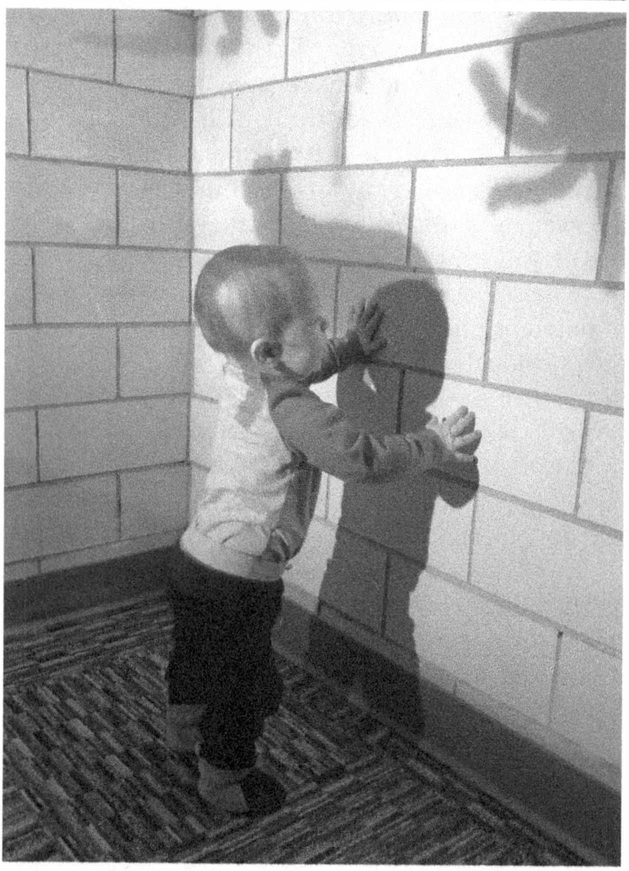

Infants first may be interested in the bulb itself and will require many opportunities for exploration before they become aware of the image on the wall or screen (see Figure 8.5). Even more experiences will be needed before these children make a connection between the OHP light and the relationships with objects and their shadows.

Plastic chains, opaque and translucent objects, and tissue paper, foil, string, yarn, or feathers sealed between laminating sheets will enable infants to manipulate materials safely as they begin to notice the images on the screen or wall. Educators can change the displays as infants begin to attend to the screen rather than the materials.

The understanding that infant educators have about each child's disposition and approaches to learning will provide them with the expertise needed to provide every child with materials that will stimulate their interest. Responsive curriculum planning should begin with a study of the individual children who are in the group so that educators

can support children's internal motivation to learn (Lally, 2005). Infants who are not yet mobile rely on adults to observe carefully and to base their actions on the children's responses. Infants' reliance on adults to choose materials, organize classroom spaces, and plan activities implies that adults must understand the possibilities for the experience before introducing it.

ITM: Providing Opportunities. Educators will discover a wide variety of light sources that will interest the children. We label some sources human-made to distinguish them from natural lights, most of which are found outdoors. These include the sun and moon, stars, and some insects. Most of our experiences with infants are with human-made sources.

Adults provide opportunities for non-mobile infants to experience light and shadow phenomena by positioning the children so that they have access to materials, while adults maintain close proximity to the infants. Materials can be placed in baskets or containers that can be grabbed, tipped, or moved easily by infants who are beginning to reach and grasp objects. Younger infants can be placed supine on the floor, on low cushions, in laps, or in a seat for support so that educators can move the light sources into their field of vision and observe the response.

Similarly, interesting designs or colored objects can be placed on an overhead projector and projected onto a screen or wall. Non-mobile infants will enjoy looking at these for a period of time. Then educators can change the design or objects to regain their interest.

TEXTBOX 8.4. JAXON AND CARLY WATCH THE DISCO LIGHT

Jaxon (12 months) and Carly (10 months) were playing in a corner of the classroom where the teacher had placed a disco light that flashed large colored dots on the wall. Jaxon moved toward the wall and got on his knees as he touched the flashing dots. His teacher asked, "Do you like those colors, Jaxon?" He stopped and turned around to look at her. He noticed Carly seated near the light source and moved toward her. The teacher scooped Carly up and moved to the wall with Carly on her lap. Carly noticed the flashing lights and crawled closer to the wall. Her teacher asked,

"Carly, did you find it?" Carly pulled to stand next to the wall and patted one of the flashing lights. Jaxon moved back to the wall near Carly and blinked several times as the lights flashed, then said, "Ooh, ooh," and moved to the wall again and began patting the dots. He then clapped his hands several times and watched the dots move. When he turned to look at the teacher, he noticed the disco light on the low table and moved toward it to look more closely (see Figure 8.6).

The infant educators described in Textbox 8.4 provided opportunities with a novel human-made light source during the Light and Shadow investigation. They had observed the infants' interest in the images displayed on the wall while investigating the OHP and wanted to capitalize on their natural curiosity with the disco light. They made the decision to provide experiences that would capitalize on the children's prior experience with a visual display.

Educators used the observations made during the previous infant explorations to determine what they might add to the Light and Shadow center. During common planning time, they heard from other educators that the young toddlers had been fascinated with the blinking lights and changing colors of the disco light and wondered whether the mobile infants would have a similar response. They determined that the corner of the classroom would allow the mobile infants to explore this new light source during a time in the morning when most of the infants were awake and active.

Educators can provide mobile infants with light and shadow materials in several places within the space reserved for play so that children can select the materials that are of interest to them and pursue this interest without interference. The Light and Shadow investigation might include containers with fairy lights and battery-operated tea lights in one area; a small, portable light pad with translucent, transparent, and opaque materials in another spot; and a basket of child-friendly flashlights. This kind of variety gives children some control over their investigation, while allowing educators to monitor the classroom and support the children.

Educators may have observed that young children often play briefly with materials, move on, and then return to these materials for further exploration. Providing space so that materials can remain available throughout a play period encourages mobile infants to return to continue their investigations.

ITM: Making Decisions. Decisions made regarding materials, space, and time are based on the educators' knowledge about infant development and the unique characteristics of infants in the classroom.

Figure 8.6. Checking Out the Disco Lights

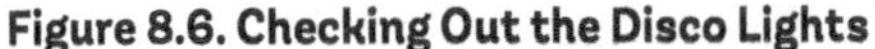

When educators document their observations of infant responses to Light and Shadow experiences and reflect on those observations, they can make informed decisions that will support children's learning. Documenting what children know and can do may include anecdotal records or a quick note jotted on a Post-it that can be attached to a clipboard for each child and collected at the end of the day. Short videos or still photos can be used for documentation and shared with parents during a conference. Some programs use apps to communicate with parents that include information about the activities infants have participated in during the day, have the capability to manage photos and video, and include developmental observations and notes.

We have observed and initiated many experiences with infants and lights, some of which we have described here. We are confident that educators who decide to explore ideas presented in this book will have additional creative ideas about how to engage and encourage infants and toddlers to explore materials.

Light and Shadow Experiences With Young Toddlers

Mobile infants and young toddlers are curious about everything and observe carefully when changes are made to the classroom. They notice a new arrangement of furniture or that the housekeeping corner has new hats and purses. They detect differences in the lighting—the amount of natural light that is streaming into the room or the way in which the human-made light is altered. This kind of subtle change in the environment is a way to start the investigation of light and shadows. What happens when the educator turns the lights down or adds a human-made light source? What do children notice about the bottles of colored water that have been placed on the shelf, when the sun is streaming into the classroom window? These are the kinds of natural provocations that can be a signal to adults that young children are ready for Light and Shadow investigations.

Light and Shadow investigations can begin simply by lowering the overhead lights and adding a blind or curtain to alter the natural light. Educators will observe the children's response and begin introducing a variety of human-made light sources. There are many child-friendly flashlights with easy-to-operate on–off switches or those that require only

squeezing or turning a handle. It is important to have enough so that all who are interested can try out a flashlight. Finding a dark place, such as a hallway with the lights off or a closet with ample space for several children, may be needed if the classroom is too bright. A blanket fort made with a low table, or a child-sized teepee or tent, will provide a popular place to investigate flashlights. Flashlights are sure to interest children, and learning to turn them on and off has a number of benefits, including fine-motor skill development and approaches to learning such as perseverance and curiosity. Providing a variety of flashlights ensures that children with differing skills can find one that they can use successfully. Educators can introduce flashlights by leaving some off and some on so that toddlers notice differences in the flashlights, such as the number of bulbs or how they are activated.

Light Tables. Light tables and the fascinating objects that accompany them will be a source of wonder for this age group. Children are delighted with the transformation of familiar classroom toys when placed on the light table. Educators can observe and document what children are drawn to, how they combine objects, and what they gather from around the room to explore on the light table. Spatial thinking will be evident as children place objects in particular ways and then move them many times before they are satisfied with the results. Attention spans at the light table may surprise educators. We observed a young toddler who was engaged at the light table for nearly 20 minutes (see Figure 8.7).

Overhead Projectors. The overhead projector is of great interest to children in this age group, and the materials selected for infant exploration also will fascinate young toddlers (see Figure 8.8). Opaque, translucent, and transparent objects as well as educator-made laminated overlays filled with interesting materials can be combined on the bed of the projector and will encourage exploration. Children first will be interested in the bulb (see Figure 8.8), as Aysha was. They gradually will begin paying attention to the bed and the surface on which the image is displayed. Given time and support, they will begin noticing how they can change the image that is projected. Educators can promote this exploration by selecting limited amounts of materials and

Figure 8.7. Exploring a Light Table

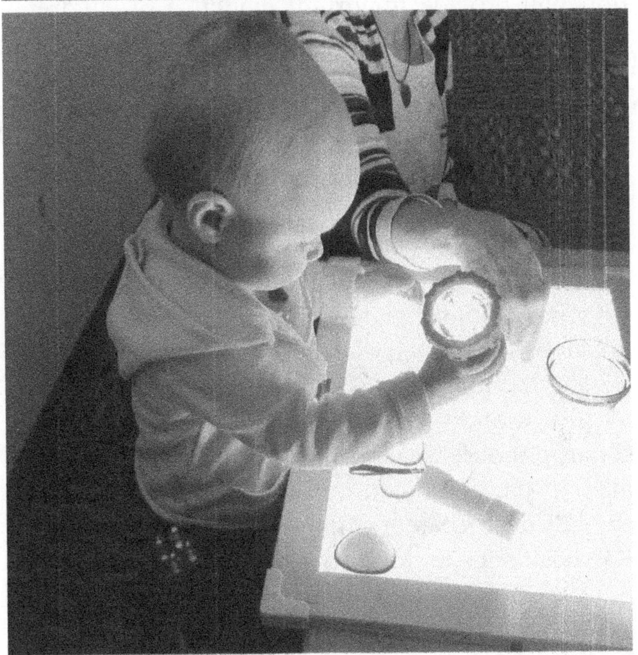

Figure 8.8. Wondering With the Overhead Projector

introducing new ones gradually as they monitor children's beginning understanding about how their actions affect the display.

ITM: Engaging Young Toddlers. Young toddlers are engaged easily when educators capitalize on their natural curiosity about how things work. Interest in the previous light investigations, as well as attention paid to developing motor skills and approaches to learning, will support exploration of flashlights and other light sources. Introducing flashlights with a variety of methods of activation will allow all children to participate in manipulating the lights. Young children need time and opportunity to explore in order to make sense of new materials that are added to their play. Allowing uninterrupted time to investigate the materials until the toddlers are satisfied with the results of their investigations also supports inquiry learning.

Many young toddlers have noticed shadows on the playground, wondered about the objects that are illuminated when placed in a window, or have been fascinated with a flashlight being used by an adult. Stimulating interest will not be difficult. Children will be eager to explore the materials that are provided, and adults will see them call upon their previous experiences with open-ended materials in order to use the flashlights, light table, and OHP. Educators

can support toddlers by observing carefully, providing intentional interventions when needed, and documenting learning as children investigate light and shadows, so educators can plan for additional experiences. They can engage young toddlers by selecting interesting materials that have been tested for safety and can be used independently by children in this age group. Trusting children to find problems they are interested in investigating rather than sticking to specific lessons, objectives, and standards enables young children to exercise their natural inclination to find out about the world and how it works.

ITM: Providing Opportunities. Educators should plan Light and Shadow explorations so children have ample time to explore the materials and figure out how they work. Young children need to repeat their actions many times in order to wonder, strategize, and resolve. We found that children in this age group maintained an interest in the materials for several weeks, although not all the toddlers were interested in these materials every day during the time they were available. Children moved back and forth among the new learning centers and their old favorites as educators observed and documented their work.

When educators plan for more than one high-interest area at a time, material and space conflicts can be minimized and children will have time to try out their ideas, use old strategies, and develop new strategies based on their own observations. Introducing the flashlights and the light table at the same time may ensure that all the children have a novel experience that they find engaging. Adding the OHP or the disco ball lights later may renew interest in the investigation.

Textbox 8.5. Valerie Solves a Problem

Valerie sat on the floor with a small hand-squeeze flashlight that she was able to turn on and off using her thumbs. She looked around her as she squeezed the flashlight and activated it. Valerie grabbed a large translucent plastic container and held her hand out to indicate that she wanted to use a closet push-light that was nearby. Valerie turned the light sideways and slipped it into the plastic container, then reached for the hand-squeeze flashlight. She turned the flashlight and slid it into the container next to the closet light. She observed the results and then tucked in the wrist strap from the squeeze light so that it was completely contained. She looked down to the floor and selected a mini LED flashlight and attempted to slip it into the space left in the container. The mini flashlight fell out, and Valerie tipped it upside down and held her hand over the opening in the container. She moved it back and forth, pulled the hand-squeeze light out by the wrist strap, then dropped it to the floor while looking at the closet light that remained in the container. She stuck her whole hand inside the container and attempted to remove the light. When she was unable to remove it by pulling, she turned the container upside down and shook it vigorously. She stopped several times to place the container in an upright position and tried to remove the light with her hand, then tipped it upside down again to shake it. The educator noticed her efforts and moved toward her to assist if she indicated that she wanted help. Valerie continued with her efforts until she had successfully removed the light.

We found that when we reintroduced the materials or added new ones, the toddlers found new ways to use them. For infant and toddler educators, this kind of experience planning rather than lesson planning demonstrates intentionality, knowledge about what is developmentally appropriate for infants and toddlers, and respect for young children as learners.

ITM: Making Decisions. Observation and reflection will provide important evidence of children's thinking, support for aligning curriculum with standards, and documentation of learning to be shared with parents, community members, and administrators. Educators can use these observations and their documentation to determine when children might need more time with the materials or a different challenge. Planning for changes to the center or additional materials will be based on these careful observations that educators make when children are actively engaged in the experience or when they notice that interest is waning.

In the above example, the educators in Valerie's classroom observed her interest in toys and materials that had a problem to be solved, such as taking the lids off containers, filling them, and putting the lids back on, or carefully stacking blocks to make a tower. These observations provided insight about what materials she might find interesting in the Light and Shadow center. The addition of containers to the flashlight tub gave her additional challenges and problems to be solved.

Light and Shadow Experiences With Older Toddlers

Older toddlers may notice their shadows on the playground and be interested in the differences and similarities between their shadow and their educator's shadow or in how their shadow is transformed when a cloud covers the sun temporarily. This may be the ideal provocation for Light and Shadow work. Children may be interested in comparing shadows, drawing around them with sidewalk chalk, or trying to step on one another's shadows while playing.

When the investigation is taken inside, older toddlers will be thrilled with an opportunity to operate a variety of child-friendly flashlights that can be placed in a center during work time. They will notice the differences and similarities in the flashlights that are available and will delight in sharing flashlights from home, which will provide a language experience activity as children share information about the light they have contributed to the center. They will transport flashlights to other centers to discover what can be illuminated with additional light. They will experience a feeling of accomplishment as they master this new technology.

Educators can make decisions by observing the way that individual children tackle the problem of turning a flashlight on or off. Does the child exhibit frustration when the flashlight is difficult to activate? Does the child seek or accept help from a trusted adult or ask a peer when it can't be figured out? Does the child try new strategies when the old ones don't work? The opportunities to see early learning standards played out are endless with this STEM experience.

Children of this age love to find places to hide, and to play in enclosed spaces. Educators can provide opportunities for investigation by making a blanket fort, obtaining an empty appliance box, or throwing a sheet over the indoor climber. A simple structure can be made with plastic pipe or a card table and an opaque curtain so that children can take their light sources inside a space that is darker than the classroom. Educators can provide additional opportunities for investigation on days when it is possible to darken the entire classroom, and on other days the "cave" can be a place for enthusiastic children to continue their work when others have moved on. Observation of child interest is necessary so that educators can determine how to facilitate exploration and activate prior knowledge for all children in STEM investigations. There may be some older toddlers who want to continue with light and shadow experiences for months.

ITM: Engaging Older Toddlers. Light tables and overhead projectors will fascinate older toddlers. Use of the same or similar materials as have been gathered for infants and young toddlers will provoke interest and investigation. Introducing at least two of the Light and Shadow interest areas simultaneously will allow all children opportunities to investigate Light and Shadow materials. Adults can alternate observation in the centers to monitor child interest, document learning, intervene to promote deeper thinking, and assist children with conflict.

and pointed to communicate her findings to her teacher (see Figure 8.9). She continued to investigate the materials, pausing each time she added something new to the bed of the OHP to observe the results of her actions. This was an example of Hilary's resolution of the problem she had posed for herself. She was satisfied with the exploration and the actions she had taken, and accepted the solution to the problem she had identified. She repeated the successful activity and demonstrated her resolution to others.

Older toddlers may be interested in the process of gathering materials. The educator can ask, "I wonder whether there is anything on the toy shelves that we could use on the light table or on the projector." Children will be eager to help and may even find objects and materials that adults had not considered for the Light and Shadow center.

Figure 8.9. Hilary Makes Shadows

ITM: Providing Opportunities. Older toddlers are beginning to demonstrate spatial understanding by using words such as *in, on, under, up,* or *down* and to follow simple directions related to these position words. Light and Shadow investigations are a perfect vehicle for children to develop understanding of these spatial concepts as well as to demonstrate awareness of their body in space. The presence of a center in the classroom where a large screen can be used with a battery-operated LED light is an invitation that older toddlers cannot resist. Educators can facilitate exploration by giving children space to investigate body shadows and can support problem solving when children experiment with the position of the light source and the screen so they can begin to understand this spatial relationship. Children of this age will need many opportunities to investigate shadows. They will be interested in using and making shadow puppets and will find hand shadows intriguing as they attempt to make things that are recognizable.

ITM: Making Decisions. Educators can check for understanding as they observe closely during Light and Shadow investigations. When educators investigate the materials before introducing them, they can be prepared to intervene with comments and questions or to sit quietly by as children grapple with self-imposed problems and find solutions that may or may not seem satisfying to us. Selective intervention takes practice, and if we learn to zip our lips until our comments and questions are sought out by children, we can avoid interrupting children's thinking and learning. This is a part of inquiry learning and teaching.

Documenting children's planning, persistence, and ability to focus attention during STEM investigations provides educators with important information about the habits of mind that are developing during these investigations with interesting and provocative materials. Providing opportunities for young children to acquire these early building blocks for STEM learning is an important challenge for infant and toddler educators. Helping children learn to plan, focus, switch gears, and think about more than one thing at a time is critical to healthy development and to becoming a lifelong learner (Center on the Developing Child, 2011).

EDUCATOR PLANNING FOR LIGHT AND SHADOW

Light and Shadow investigations require an inventory of the environment and careful observation of the natural light during various times of the day. Planning for the use of the available lighting during optimal learning periods for the children also implies that educators may need to alter the schedule or group children according to their daily routines. The planning process necessitates establishing a learning environment that accounts for what we know about the individual needs and temperaments of the children who will be engaging in the experience.

Planning for the Infant Environment

As educators begin to plan for this learning experience, there are likely to be several factors to take into consideration regarding the physical, invitational, and temporal environments. In infant classrooms, it may be necessary to plan for the needs of infants from 4 weeks to 1 year. Cribs for sleeping cannot be stacked or stored and must be available throughout the day. Individual daily schedules will change from month to month as the youngest infants begin to be awake for longer periods and older infants begin to move independently. In many programs, infants arrive and depart throughout the day, so scheduling interest centers may include only part of the group. All these factors must be taken into consideration when educators begin to plan for Light and Shadow work and determine how they will adjust the natural light and arrange the human-made light sources.

Planning for the Toddler Environment

Throughout the Light and Shadow investigation, educators may need to modify the room arrangement, adjust the schedule, or amend the experiences planned for the day to take advantage of available light. Educators can ask questions, collaborate with teaching partners, and brainstorm after observations with the various light sources to develop an optimal learning environment for exploring light and shadow.

Planning for the Light and Shadow experiences also requires that educators take inventory of the available materials, gather materials from other classrooms, scrounge some materials that were stored or had been discarded, ask families to save or donate materials, and purchase some items that are determined to be necessary for the experience. Throughout the planning process, educators can refer to resources that are available on social media, in curriculum planning guides, or from the successful experiences that other educators share. One invaluable resource for choosing infant and toddler materials and introducing them is *Infants and Toddlers at Work: Using Reggio-Inspired Materials to Support Brain Development* (Lewin-Benham, 2010).

Materials and Equipment

Educators can take a mental inventory of the materials in their setting. What materials are already present that could be used for Light and Shadow investigations? Which materials would be safe for infants and toddlers to use? Many classrooms have loose parts such as plastic buttons, wooden shapes, glass beads, or a variety of transparent, translucent, or opaque objects that are large enough for infant and toddler exploration. Other materials that often can be found in infant and toddler classrooms are wooden unit blocks, magnetic tiles, scarves, puppets, or large farm or zoo animals. Families may be willing to save their recyclables or contribute materials, even temporarily, that will lend themselves to exploration, such as LED work lights from the garage, flashlights from a camping trip, or an old shower curtain liner to be used as a screen. Educators can use ribbons, paper scraps, and tissue paper to make laminated overlays for the overhead projector.

Educators should be intentional in the selection of materials so that the interests and abilities of all learners can be addressed. Materials provide immediate connections between the brain and the environment (Lewin-Benham, 2010). Keeping essential goals in mind when selecting materials will assist educators in finding a variety of materials that will engage children and provide opportunities for them to engage in science, technology, engineering, and math while developing receptive and expressive language.

Safety is the prime consideration when choosing materials, and educators must try out all the light sources before introducing them to make sure they do not give off excess heat. LED lights can be used safely, as they remain cool to the touch for an extended period of use. In addition, for these younger children adults must check any objects daily to be certain they pass the choke test.

Button batteries can be poisonous if swallowed, so it is important to find a way to make the lights with these batteries (such as tea lights) inaccessible to the children. Placing them inside a clear lidded container can allow children to use the materials safely.

A Closer Look at Materials to Consider for Light and Shadow

Below we list some materials that will be especially helpful in supporting the children's exploration of light and shadows. All materials should be examined carefully before offering them to the children. Finding funding to support procuring appropriate materials was discussed in the previous chapter.

- Overhead projector: An OHP combines a magnifying lens, a projecting lens, a light source, and a bed. When children place items on the bed of the projector, they can create and manipulate light and shadows on a screen or wall. An OHP can be hard to find, but some schools have a few hidden away in storage closets. We sent out an appeal to other departments at our university and found a few that had been stored. We also found them on eBay, but we were lucky to get ours at no cost. Some companies manufacture an updated version of the overhead projector.
- Light table or light pad: We used a stand-alone light table with the older toddlers, but found the small, portable light pads designed for artist use to be best, as they could be moved to various places in the room and took up little space.
- Wall washer: A wall washer–type of light "washes" a wall or part of a wall with illumination rather than shining a focused beam on one particular area or downward toward the floor. When a wall washer is used, it illuminates the vertical surfaces and enables play with shadows without completely darkening the room. Wall washers come in sizes with a variety of

lumens. We purchased a wall washer with a remote control that allowed us to change colors with the touch of a button. Some families may have wall washers that are used for holidays to light up an outdoor display. Educators should experiment with these before introducing them to determine the amount of heat produced.

- Large screen (made with a frame of PVC pipes and sturdy white fabric) with wooden or binder clips to attach it at the top. We also made a simple screen with a shower curtain liner and clips attached to a clothesline in a doorway. Finding a spot where the children can be in front of the screen or behind it, rather than displaying the light on a flat wall, offers expanded opportunities for exploration.
- Small screen (made from Plexiglas) with wooden "feet" to hold it in place on a low table
- Blackout curtains for windows and door
- Small LED flashlights with simple on–off button
- Medium-sized flashlights made for children
- Closet push-lights
- Rechargeable LED lights
- Battery-operated fairy lights placed inside clear containers with sealed lids
- Keychain lights
- Mini Maglites
- Disco ball light: A disco ball is a spherical object that reflects light directed at it in many directions, producing a complex display. Our disco light was "found" material that was stashed in a classroom cupboard. It was handheld rather than mounted, so it required an adult to hold it and move it for the infants and toddlers. Newer versions are available from various online sources.
- A variety of transparent and translucent containers with lids, including clear mailing tubes, plastic shoeboxes with clear lids, food storage containers with clear lids, and zippered clear bags such as those used for blankets or curtains. Again, plastic containers require good adult supervision to keep children safe from asphyxiation.
- Small laminated sheets with feathers, tissue paper, ribbon, and string pressed inside to use on OHP and light table (these were educator-made).

Educators and children will find additional interesting materials to explore as they become more familiar with light and shadows, both indoors and outside. We believe that educators will become more creative in producing or acquiring materials as they spend more time in inquiry learning and teaching because the children will inspire them.

For very young children, scientific inquiry unfolds naturally as they engage in open-ended experiences in which they create problems for themselves and try to seek out solutions to them. Young children can make observations and predictions, carry out simple investigations, collect data, and begin to understand what they have discovered (McClure et al., 2017).

Adults can support infant-toddler inquiry learning with light and shadows when they plan experiences with interesting materials that can be safely explored. We encourage educators to share these new experiences with children by observing and supporting rather than directing, and to find ways to help the children to make sense of the discoveries by connecting them to previous learning.

Infant and toddler educators should be cognizant of the fact that children figure things out by repeating actions and making sense of the world and how it works. We cannot hurry this process. Our responsibility to young children requires that we give them time to solve their own problems by engaging in exploration and investigation in a safe and nurturing environment that honors their individual learning strengths and challenges, their unique characteristics, and their culture and community.

CHAPTER 9

Exploring Sound With Infants and Toddlers

Sonia Yoshizawa and Sherri Peterson

TEXTBOX 9.1. MARTIN MAKES A SHAKER

Thirty-month-old Martin picked up three small die-cast cars and put them one by one inside a small plastic canister. Each time he dropped a car in the container, he closed the lid, shook the container, and shouted, "BIG shaker!" He walked around the classroom looking for more cars. He spotted several small cars in a bowl near the block center and carried the bowl, smiling, to his corner. Noticing that the bowl of cars went missing, Jalen stood up at the block center and approached Martin. "What you doin'?" Jalen asked. Martin pointed at the canister with cars inside. "Making BIG shaker!" he confidently voiced, using big hand gestures to express his excitement. "Shaker???" Curious, Jalen leaned over to see Martin's canister, half-full of die-cast cars, and asked, "Shaker? Can I try?" Jalen grabbed a handful of cars from the bowl and threw them inside the canister. Martin put the lid on, and shook. "Big, BIG shaker!" Martin shouted in excitement, and both children started laughing. "Let's put more!" Jalen suggested. Still laughing, Martin and Jalen threw the rest of the cars inside the canister until it was full to the brim. They placed the lid on the container and shook. No noise this time. They shook it again, but no sound came from the canister. The boys looked at each other, seeming confused. Martin opened the lid, closed it again, and shook. The educator, who had been quietly observing this intriguing children-initiated sound project, intervened. "What happened to the big shaker? I remember seeing Martin shake and make a LOUD noise." She smiled. Jalen and Martin opened the lid again, removed a couple of cars, put the lid back on, and shook. "I hear some soft noise now . . . I see you both removed a few cars?" The educator carefully described their actions and used the correct terms—*loud* and *soft*—and gave just enough comment to scaffold the children's problem solving. Martin and Jalen immediately dumped several cars out of the canister, placed the lid back on, and shook. "BIG noise again! I made BIG shaker!" Jalen supported this idea and said, "I made loud noise [shaker], too!"

Playing with sound is a familiar practice in every known culture and at every age level in the history of humankind (Armstrong, 2019). With infants, the very first sound play you observe as an educator may take the form of vocal play—learning to use the tongue, lips, gums, and jaw to make noises, which provide the foundation for oral communication. Study results show a significant increase in developmentally advanced, consonant–vowel vocalizations, which represent the connection between babbling and the formation of words, when an educator responds positively to infants' babbling or cooing sounds (Gros-Louis et al., 2014). As children develop vocal play, it becomes just one of the ways that children engage in sound exploration. Sound may be produced outside their bodies, such as holding and dropping a metal spoon on a wooden floor, shaking a rattle, or striking a xylophone bar with a mallet (see Figure 9.1). Notice how toddlers Martin and Jalen created sound from several die-cast cars and explored one of the components of sound—loudness—while also finding out that the word "big" in music means "loud." They also predicted how they could make a loud sound but found that filling up the canister with more cars did not lead to an amplified sound. Repeated experiences like this encourage children's autonomy,

Figure 9.1. Striking a Xylophone

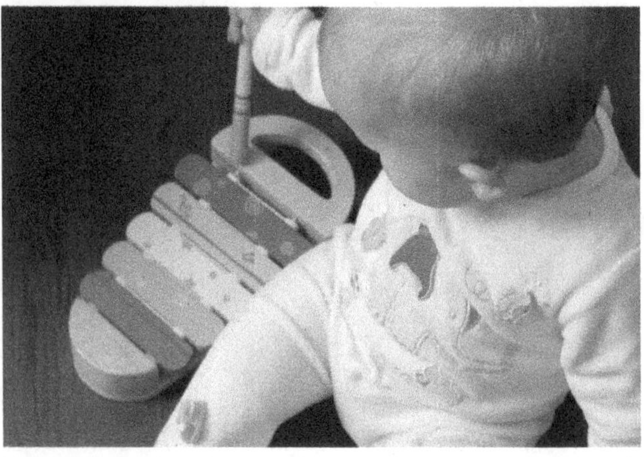

Exploring sound is a physical science activity that offers a wide range of possibilities to develop auditory skills in young children. Auditory skills lay an important foundation that prepares children to build listening and communication skills, as well as understanding sound as music. The ability to detect, identify, differentiate, and modify sound, in addition to interpreting that sound can be beautiful and harmonious or merely a collection of clashing sounds, is a critical skill that affects the overall development of a child's brain.

In science, sound is defined as a type of energy made by vibrations. This means that anything that carries the sound, including air and water, results in creating a tone that may be intriguing to young ears. Children may be surprised at a unique sound quality, such as the voice of a stranger, a rhythmic sound of a bullfrog on a summer night, or a train whistle that may startle their sensitive ears. For children with hearing impairment or deafness, sound can be felt or seen—by touching the surface of a speaker with loud, ongoing music or seeing ripples and splashes of water when striking a tuning fork and placing it just above the water's surface (Hildebrandt & Zan, 2002). Listening to a repertoire of sound and music early in their lives impacts children's biological, cognitive, and emotional well-being, resulting in an increased ability to learn new and complex things and activate all areas of the growing brain (Mehegan & Rainville, 2020). Offering sound activity to young children helps the whole brain, not just a specific area of the brain. It is a brain workout!

drive them to investigate further how the physical world works, and support them when developing new strategies for making something interesting happen. In the process, children also learn that different actions result in different outcomes, which is fundamental in STEM learning.

WHY SOUND WITH INFANTS AND TODDLERS?

Development of a human brain is fascinating. Researchers at the Center on the Developing Child at Harvard University describe how neural connections for different functions develop sequentially (Center on the Developing Child, 2007). The sensory pathways, such as hearing, grow while the child is inside the mother's womb, and by the 25th week of pregnancy, the baby is already responding to familiar noises and voices. This means that when babies are born, their hearing is "on" and ready to embrace all types of sound in their environment, which is why you may have heard that the early years are extremely important for language development. Neuroscientists warn, though, that this remarkable period when babies can hear and learn all types of sounds does not last forever (Kraus & Slater, 2015; Kuhl, 2010a). The critical window for connecting and distinguishing one speech sound from another closes around 13 months. Before this window closes, the brain starts pruning the sounds that children do not hear regularly. In other words, a single, brief conversation spoken in a language different from the baby's home language will not be registered in the baby's brain.

INFANT TODDLER INQUIRY LEARNING MODEL WITH SOUND EXPLORATION

With infants and toddlers who have not yet received formal music training, educators may notice their wondering about sound-producing objects rather than playing a fine-tuned musical instrument (see Figure 9.2), a skill that develops much later. An infant tapping two blocks against each other, or a toddler walking around the room striking other objects with a spoon, are examples of sound exploration. Many times, this type of exploration begins without intention. For example, an accidental drop of a plastic sippy cup on the floor may lead to a series of repetitive intentional drops, especially if there is an

Figure 9.2. Wondering About Sound

adult involved in picking up the cup and handing it back to the infant.

Instead of quickly judging that the child is playing a game of patience with you, it is important to note that this drop may result in several different discoveries for the child, sound being one of them. We suggest educators be open-minded observers for many possibilities during the process of exploration.

Narges appeared to be wondering about the difference in the sounds she created when tapping the hard surface with her chalk (see Figure 9.3). She strategized by making three types of sounds: one when she tapped holding the chalk diagonally, another when she used the tip of the chalk while holding it vertically, and finally when she tapped one piece of chalk against another. Narges then tapped three times with a fast beat. Although we can only guess what she was thinking, it is safe to say that Narges was exploring the properties of the chalk and the paper on the table, the different sounds she

Figure 9.3. Narges Taps the Chalk

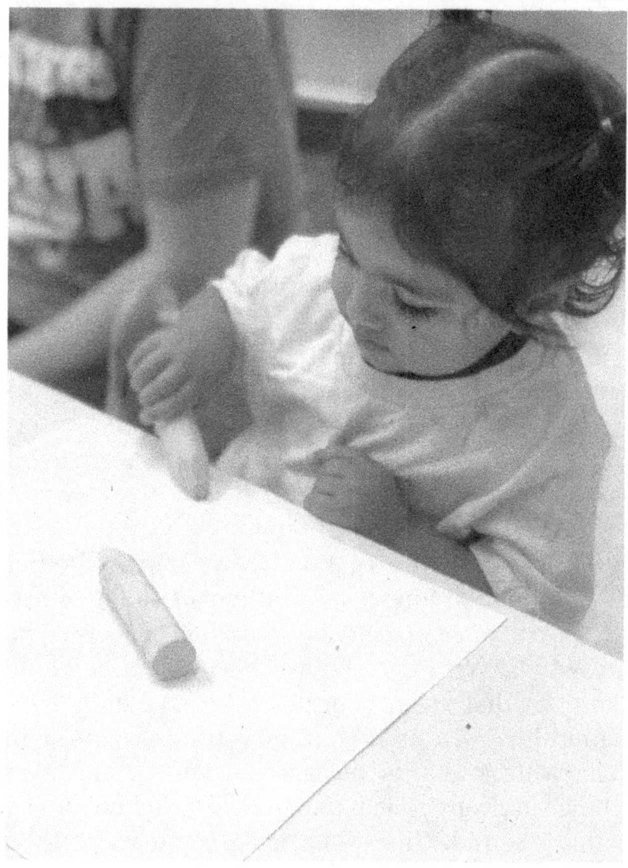

made when she varied the impact of the taps, and how changing her grasp altered the sound when she tapped at different angles. For the time being, she resolved her wondering.

An interesting observation was made from the perspective of Narges's educator, Melissa, who believed Narges was beginning to take an interest in writing. Melissa immediately interpreted this as the beginning skills of literacy and provided an important perspective about observation and interpretation. Again, we can only guess what Narges was thinking as she explored with the chalk and paper. Was she noticing the dots and lines on the paper that the chalk made as she tapped? Was she listening to the sounds made with the chalk and strategizing about how she could make a new sound? When educators document experiences like this one and then reflect on the observation, they can keep their eyes and ears open to all possibilities. Collaborating with other adults who are documenting learning in the classroom can help to take another perspective about what children are doing. With infants and toddlers who have limited communication skills, educators base their assessment on observation, on knowledge of children, and through the relationships that are formed. The more you know the child, the better you will understand the child's interests, personality, habits, and learning as they continue to construct their knowledge.

INQUIRY TEACHING MODEL WITH SOUND

Offering an intentional learning environment where young children can explore sound, be autonomous, and be empowered to practice free inquiry may feel like an overwhelming assignment for educators. Where do we begin? If every object has the possibility of producing a sound when used in a certain way, how do we know whether a child will be interested in the material(s) educators prepare (e.g., Narges's chalk and paper)? The answer is: We do not know. However, what we do know is that as an educator, you have built a relationship with each child in your classroom, and you will be able to recognize when a child takes the chalk from your hand and works on creating a unique sound, chooses to notice the marks on the

paper and creates more, or puts the chalk in their mouth! In this example with Narges, the educator had a strong connection with the child, and therefore the trust between them allowed the child to explore the possibilities and to wonder, strategize, and resolve safely and confidently under the educator's observation and supervision. Building strong connections in the classroom leads to the feelings of security, confidence, and competence to take risks necessary to learning (Dombro et al., 2011; National Research Council, 2001). We encourage educators to spend significant time building this connection with children, observe them carefully, trust them as learners, and reflect with colleagues about how this relationship can contribute to learning. This reflection and collaboration support your understanding of children's needs, interests, and preferences.

Sound Exploration With Infants

For young infants who are not yet mobile and mostly dependent on the educator for exploratory activities, adults can start by preparing a repertoire of background music collected from selected music genres for their classroom. Keep in mind that the music you will play in the background has a purpose, so the type of music you select, when you will play it, and how often you vary it are critical choices you make intentionally. Some common misconceptions for educators are that children need to have music playing all the time, that music labeled as children's songs is the only choice, and that lullabies or classical music should be played when children are napping. Adults should remember that these songs were not labeled or chosen by children themselves.

Educators may be surprised to learn that some lullaby lyrics have an underlying political or historical meaning that may not be appropriate for children. Instead of choosing music that is labeled as children's music, create a music library based on tempo, or the speed or pace at which a passage of music is played. Slow, instrumental music could be played during naptime and downtime. The ambient music or calming music you enjoy at night can be a perfect replacement for a lullaby. Volume is also very important, so test the speakers in the classroom or the playing device before you play for the children. And, of course, if you enjoy singing or humming,

Figure 9.4. Music Genres and Suggestions When to Play for Infants and Toddlers

Music Genres	When to Play
Soft and Slow (instrumental, no lyrics) • Environmental music • Ambient music • Meditation music • Calming or healing music **Note:** These types of music have no beginning or ending, and no repetition of recognizable parts, making the music continuous and playable for a longer period of time. **Note:** If playing instrumental music, switch instrument type (e.g., piano, guitar, flute, violin, cello, etc.) to offer a variety of sound sources.	• Naptime • Bottle-feeding time • Quiet time • Relaxing time • Snack time • Listening time **Note:** Be mindful not to play this type of music throughout the day. While music can be soothing, it is important to have pauses, or a silent time for children. Remember that a type of music that is comforting for you may not translate the same for some children. Please observe them carefully for their reaction when you play music, especially as background music.
Moderate to Upbeat (instrumental, no lyrics) • Jazz • Bossa nova, soft samba • Celtic • Classical • Reggae • Country, blues • Music from various cultures/countries • Music focused on specific instrument(s) • Creative music played with unique instrument(s)	• Active time • Focus time • Snack time • Free play time **Note:** All genres introduced here should be played intentionally and not as background music.
Variety (with lyrics) • Children's songs • Musicals • Soundtrack music • Folk songs	• Awake time • Sing-along • Music and movement • Reading **Note:** These songs are appropriate to play during planned participation time.

know that your voice would be a wonderful addition to your music repertoire.

As a contrast, create an upbeat tempo music collection to play when children are active (see Figure 9.4). Moderation is recommended, as playing heavy metal music, or classical music pieces with loud cymbals, bells, and trumpets, may confuse children. Songs with lyrics are not discouraged, but begin with instrumental music, and include music from different cultures, rhythms, and instruments. Have you tried playing bolero, a soft samba, reggae, or a waltz? Children also may be intrigued with a beautiful song played with a handpan (Figure 9.5), a percussion instrument made of steel, or a Celtic harp.

Educators should be intentional about the music choices and the times when they are played. In addition, adults need to remember that there are times when constant music can make some children uncomfortable. Some children with special needs may prefer a quieter time and space in the environment. Offering a quiet time also allows children to explore and hear softer sounds that may be drowned out by loud music.

Finding music to play in your classroom should be a fun project for educators. Taking some time to collect the music you will play in your classroom includes making sure you listen to the entire song before adding it to the list. The purpose for this music collection is to expose children to a variety of sounds and music and is not to be confused with teaching vocabulary, counting, naming body parts, actions, or other academic skills using music as a platform. Educators can plan for other times to use these skill-building songs, but be aware that these are entirely different purposes.

Providing a listening repertoire of music will assist with one dimension of sound exploration, which is the ability to hear and distinguish different types of sounds coming from instruments or

Figure 9.5. Handpan

materials that produce sound. King Lear, a famous character in William Shakespeare's play, said to his daughter Cordelia that "nothing comes from nothing." The same idea can be applied when building critical thinking skills in STEM. Infants would not be able to be creative problem-solvers if they did not have prior experiences that helped develop these skills. An infant may grasp a rattle, but if the child never learns to shake, the rattle may never become a sound or a sensory instrument. If the child had prior experience shaking, the knowledge could be applied so that they could solve the problem successfully by shaking the rattle.

ITM: *Engaging Infants.* Providing a safe environment where infants can engage with sound-producing materials starts small but is always intentional. Adults can take the children's perspective by thinking of their size and imagine how they may move. Educators can make sure there is plenty of space for them to reach, crawl, sit up, and walk. Starting with a few materials that are open-ended, and with many possibilities to explore, will set the stage. Providing only commercial (and expensive) musical instruments may limit these possibilities, so we suggest that you invest in quality and focus on the varied sound

effects materials produce when they are explored. For example, the chalk Narges was using may not be safe if placed in the mouth, but it provided different sound effects when tapped in a certain way. Wooden blocks, metal or wooden canisters, or tin cans in conjunction with mallets or utensils to strike, tap, or rub would create a variety of sound effects and sounds. Be mindful that sound is not just about making a soft or loud noise. There is also a quality related to the sound. Inviting children to explore, perceive, differentiate, and reflect on their cause-and-effect actions would be an excellent opportunity to help them focus on hearing, and encourage them to investigate more possibilities with making sound.

Repeating experiences with materials that make sound also supports development of children's tonal memory in music. That is, they learn and remember that a particular sound (or tone) was made by certain materials or musical instruments so that they can recreate the sound later. Tonal memory helps with staying in tune and may be developed through ear training. This is how you may recall a favorite piece of music or song from your childhood or from last week and sing the melody in tune.

Figure 9.6 represents a creative setting of sound materials infants can safely explore while sitting on

Figure 9.6. A PVC Stand for Exploring Sounds

the floor. The educator created a PVC stand that is practical, sturdy, and safe to use for hanging sound-producing materials. Convenient plastic math links, which are affordable and washable, and easily added or reduced to adjust their height, were used to hang the materials. Notice the order and the careful spacing between the muffin pan and the kitchen utensils used as strikers, so children have ample space to move around and explore each material. Some children may prefer exploring the materials with their left hands, rather than their right, so place the materials so that both hands can be used to explore. The activity area should not be cluttered or crowded so the sound easily can be heard by the child, such as the sound of a muffin pan being struck with a utensil. In the image, bongos, which produce two high-pitched contrasting sounds, and a drum also were added. These combinations of instruments, including kitchen utensils, provide multiple possibilities for curious children to act on objects and wonder about the world of sound.

Even if infants are nonverbal, educators can wonder with children, expressing emotions with face and gestures, and using vocabulary that supplements children's exploration. If a child makes a unique sound, for example, striking a tin can with a metal spoon or plucking a guitar chord, smile or express surprise to encourage exploration. Provide materials that are appropriate for their motor skills (see Figure 9.7). Be firm if the sound activity takes a different path, such as using the strikers to hit another child, or using a metal spoon or another musical instrument to hit the drum, which may significantly damage the instrument. Redirect gently or quickly assess the environment to see whether children are sitting too close to one another or whether there are too many materials for children to navigate. If so, declutter the space or reposition the infant. Modeling how to hold the materials, how to make the sound, and ways to be careful with sound-producing materials will support children later as they learn how to handle materials and respect musical instruments.

ITM: Providing Opportunities. Hadiya is an experienced infant educator. She has a set of twins in her class who are experiencing attachment issues. While one twin is fine after their mother leaves in the morning, Mia, a 10-month-old girl, has a hard time drying her tears. Hadiya holds Mia until she settles down and walks around the classroom, passing by the window that has special items she hung there just for Mia. This routine has helped Mia regain her smile.

Figure 9.7. A Variety of Materials for Making Sound

Hadiya hung wind chimes she brought from home. The wind chimes had five long copper tubes and a wind catcher in the center, which Mia could hold and shake gently (see Photograph 9.8).

Hadiya first modeled how she could gently shake the wind catcher by pulling the center cord of the wind chimes. A beautiful combination of sound was heard when she shook the wind catcher, and she observed Mia's sudden reaction, burying her face on her chest. Mia was still crying, but quickly looked at the chimes again. Hadiya did not hesitate to smile, and said, "Mia, what a beautiful sound! Would you like to try?" Her question made Mia stop her crying, and she reached out to the wind chimes as if she was asking Hadiya to step closer. Mia shook one tube, and Hadiya tilted her head to listen, smiled, exclaimed, "This sound reminds me of the beginning part of Old MacDonald's song!," and she started singing, "Old MacDonald had a farm. . . ." Mia reached out to the wind chimes again, this time shaking them firmly and shouting, "E-I-E-I . . . U!!!" Hadiya and Mia laughed and Mia repeated, "E-I-E-I . . . Uuuu!"

This vignette is an example of an educator providing an opportunity for the child to explore a new phenomenon while strengthening her bonding with the child. Hadiya, knowing Mia's morning routine, resolved her separation anxiety issue by combining a new and positive experience that Mia could enjoy. The serve-and-return (Center on the Developing Child, 2021) interaction between these two, when Hadiya showed Mia her appreciation of the wind-chime sound, and when the child responded by reaching out, demonstrates how important the building of relationships is when children indicate curiosity and choose to investigate something new. In their short period of bonding, the educator also expressed her interest in the beautiful sound and connected the single sound of a wind-chime tube to a familiar song they both knew. At the end of the experience, they both sang "Old MacDonald," with Mia completing the ending of the song. This is an example of how observation and knowledge of the child serve as powerful tools for encouraging children to try out new opportunities, learning vocabulary, improving communication, and enhancing the adult–child relationship.

ITM: Making Decisions. Hadiya has seen many children like Mia. She did not bring wind chimes from home and other materials just to distract Mia when she was having a hard time separating from her parent. Mia has observed the twins extensively,

Figure 9.8. Wind Chimes

as she observes all of the children in her classroom. Educators who reflect on children's actions are collecting information from them continually and understand how to use the information when making decisions. Selecting a sound instrument for Mia and deciding how and where to hang the wind chimes, how often to refer to them, and which music to sing are some examples of decisions the educator made, based on her knowledge of the child. Decisions often must be made quickly, such as the choice of song when Mia rang one of the wind-chime tubes. In this case the sound of the wind chimes prompted Hadiya to remember Mia's favorite song. Educators must be prepared to make on-the-spot decisions throughout the day.

As children become more mobile, replacing materials that will continue to engage them also may require this kind of quick decision-making.

Some decisions do not require urgent modification or an immediate response and can be made after thorough observation, reflection, and collaboration with colleagues. Being open to new discoveries and approaches will get easier with practice.

In sound exploration experiences, we have observed educators asking children whether the sound they are making is soft or loud, high or low. We also have observed educators who praise children when a sound is made. Instead, the educator can listen carefully and make specific comments or ask informed questions about how the sound was made or why the child has chosen particular materials rather than others. Noticing these patterns and preferences will enable you to make rich decisions to help children learn even more.

Sound Exploration With Young Toddlers

Young toddlers continue to be curious. While pursuing the wonder of sound exploration in their classroom, educators will start noticing signs that children have sound preferences. They begin to identify sounds that are pleasant (consonant) and unpleasant (dissonant). They also may begin to vocalize a melody or a partial lyric, or hum, which may be a mixture of known and made-up songs and rhythms. If a child is from another culture, and the family plays or performs music from their culture, you may see expanded preferences and appreciation for certain types of sound, melody, rhythm, and materials that make sounds. For example, a child born in Nashville, TN, surrounded by family members who play string instruments such as violin (fiddle), banjo, or base, may find it surprising to see a musician playing a saxophone on the streets of New Orleans, LA. It is important to know that culture and environment affect the way a child appreciates music. Therefore, being open-minded about music is important for educators.

What most educators in the United States or other Western cultures may consider to be a happy song (upbeat, fast, major-scale melody) may be the equivalent of a sad song in other cultures. Knowing the background and culture of the children in your classroom and communicating with families about their preferences in music may help you better prepare sound materials that will spark curiosity, be unique, and challenge children to explore. When children's sound preferences are considered as educators plan sound experiences, children may explore sound-producing materials more attentively and develop preferences that expand focus time.

With young toddlers, educators will begin to notice how children will bring their previous sound experiences to the classroom. These sounds could be created or learned at home or from their toys, siblings, the songs they hear on TV or their electronic devices, or a grandparent who loves to sing and play an instrument. Whatever the sound source may be, we can continue to offer a wide range of sound and music genres for listening, and invite children to make music, explore materials that make different sounds, play musical instruments, move rhythmically, and sing along. Figure 9.9 will provide you with some ideas for music genres that can be used effectively with infants and toddlers.

ITM: *Engaging Young Toddlers.* As young toddlers gain more confidence with movement, they also will become more active with their sound exploration. They will select materials of their preference, collect them, and transport them to other areas in the classroom to explore. At this age, they are still not playing often with friends, but they are aware of people, especially the adults around them. As you prepare and offer intentional sound materials to young children in their environment, keep in mind that children need to be autonomous and creative, but they still need you around. You may position yourself in closer proximity to the children but refrain from intervening when they are deeply engaged. Your role is always to be a keen observer and a supportive facilitator who scaffolds only when necessary.

Many educators wonder what questions to ask when they notice children ready for additional challenges. Some feel the urge to teach, and rush to ask questions to check children's knowledge when showing a musical instrument to the child: "Can you play a loud/soft sound?" or "What is this called?" These are examples of questions that will not facilitate inquiry. Instead, being there in the moment will support what children are doing. Nonverbal feedback can be supportive of children. Questions do not always have to be verbal. Nodding your head to the beat if the children are patting the drum to maintain the beat provides feedback. Opening your eyes wide when you hear a loud sound, or tilting your head when you hear a soft sound, is responsive to the sounds children make. Closing your eyes and smiling if you enjoy the song will encourage them to continue playing. Engaging children by tapping a drum using call-and-response involves

Figure 9.9. Classification of Musical Instruments and Equivalent Materials for Exploration

Classification of Instruments	Examples of Musical Instruments	Affordable Instruments or Materials That Can Be Purchased or Assembled
Aerophones (sound is produced by the vibration of air)	Trumpet, flute, horn, accordion, whistle, clarinet, saxophone	Recorder, ocarina, glass bottle flute, pan flute with straws, PVC pipe w/holes drilled, bamboo pipe, vegetable instruments
Idiophones (sound is created by the instrument as a whole, vibrating without strings or membranes)	Cymbals, kalimba, bell, gong, triangle, maracas, castanets, wood block, glockenspiel, xylophone, handpan	Wind chimes, washboard, cowbell, rattles, castanets, blocks, bells, guiro/scraper, shakers, pots and pans, metal or aluminum lids
Membranophones (sound is made by the vibration of strings or caused by friction)	Drum, snare drum, bongos, djembe, timpani, tambourine, kazoo, some gongs, mirliton	Tin can drum, straw kazoo, comb and paper kazoo
Chordophones (sound is made by the vibration of strings)	Dulcimer, harp, harpsichord, piano, guitar, ukulele, violin, viola, base, cello, lute, banjo, autoharp	Juice carton guitar, canjo (one-string guitar made of can), autoharp, dulcimer
Electrical (sound is made by electronic or mechanical means)	Keyboard, synthesizer, electric organ, theremin, drum machine	Children's toy run by battery or electrically charged containing mechanical sound and syncopated rhythms

letting the child tap the drum first, with the adult repeating the child's sound right after. These actions soon will involve the child in an engaging musical conversation without uttering a word.

Asking verbal, open-ended questions will increase their vocabulary or demonstrate your support and appreciation. However, educators should limit praising children just because they rang a bell or strummed a few guitar chords by accident. This includes clapping your hands or saying "Good job!" every time they make a sound or noise. The child will interpret your response as praise and will repeat the action to please you or entice you to respond. To avoid this, observe children carefully when they make their sound discoveries. Are they surprised? Curious? Confused? Scared? Sometimes the noise they make startles them because it was unexpected. If they are curious and make the sound again, they are on to something! Give them time and space to explore. Give them nonverbal feedback if they look at you, but focus on giving them time to think and reflect and do it all over again. If they come to you for approval or some type of feedback, then simply encourage them by saying, "Can I hear you play it again?" or "Show me what you did (to the drum) to make that sound." Your genuine interest may encourage them to refocus and explore once again. Be their audience and enjoy listening to their process of sound-making, or be an understanding supporter if children decide to take a break and walk away from their materials.

ITM: Providing Opportunities. Providing opportunities that enrich exploration sometimes can be as spontaneous as the example of Steve and his father. Notice that this sound exploration did not happen in the classroom, but the father and son story reminds us that learning takes place at any time during the day. Whether children are outdoors like Steve, or indoors with educators, friends, or family, the opportunities often present themselves if we recognize them.

Textbox 9.4. Steve Drums the Water

Sixteen-month-old Steve was at the swimming pool having a great time with his father. They had been at the swimming pool several times to take advantage of the summer weather. Steve enjoyed splashing water randomly with his hands while his dad held him in the water. On one occasion, Steve focused on splashing the water with both hands (see Figure 9.10). Steve splashed twice with his right hand, causing a soft and gentle splashing noise. Then with his left hand, he hit the water hard, making a loud, splashing noise. Steve squealed. He repeated the pattern, softly splashing the water twice with his right hand, then hitting the water surface harder with his left hand. Steve's father intervened and said, "You made a loud sound!" Steve paused briefly and responded, "Close ears!" and went back to his splashing pattern with water.

When Steve responded to his father asking him to "close [his] ears," we understand that Steve connected the relationship between the loud sound, when he hit the water surface hard, and the soft sound, when he tapped the water surface gently. Steve's reasoning about protecting his father's ears from the loud sound, even if it is not possible to "close" his ears, demonstrated evidence that his focus was sound dynamics and not the water movement. Observing children in depth and learning their interests and challenges prepares parents and educators for unexpected learning opportunities that benefit the child. Opportunities may happen anywhere and at any time during the day.

ITM: Making Decisions. Decision-making may be a daunting task for novice educators. It can be scary, especially if the activity, such as sound, is not visible.

Figure 9.10. Making Sounds Everywhere

How do you know you are documenting the actual thoughts of the child when all you see is a child stirring a metal pot with a silicone spoon? How do you know that the child is hearing the differences of sound and comparing them when the child throws the silicone spoon away and picks up the metal spoon instead? The answer is, again, observation. If your child is stirring the pot with a silicone spoon, which makes less sound than the metal spoon, and throws it away to pick up the metal spoon, observe how long the child stirs the pot with the metal spoon. Does the child look satisfied? Does the child look up to seek attention about the discovery of loud noise? Does the child look surprised to hear the difference? If you are unsure, we suggest you try it yourself. Be the curious child and pick up a silicone spoon and a metal spoon and stir the pot yourself. You may be mesmerized by how it sounds and how it feels when an object is vibrating in your hand! A new idea may emerge, using a wooden spoon, for example. We suggest that you video-record the child's actions with the materials, if possible. When you record the child's actions and reactions, you can revisit the moment many times before making any decisions. You may discover detailed information that you missed the first time you watched the video. Sharing your video with colleagues may generate different opinions or comments. By creating a community of reflective practitioners, you will gain experience and feel confident about your thinking. What you decide next will come naturally when you can get inside the children's heads. Keep in mind that when making a decision, information about your children comes from a collection of bits and pieces you have gathered through the year, and not at the moment of your activity. Eventually, you will feel your classroom children are like your own and will know their interests, likes and dislikes, habits, when to challenge, and when to make or not to make important decisions. You will feel good about your knowledge of the children and know when to respect, nurture, and offer them further challenges.

Sound Exploration With Older Toddlers

Older toddlers who are more verbal and communicate with peers about their discoveries and challenges are marvelous to observe. They constantly are finding unique ways to build their knowledge.

Sometimes they prefer to focus entirely on their own, sitting at a corner for more than 40 minutes, trying to figure out an orchestra of sound variables with found materials to replicate the memories they may have from watching a concert or a band. With older toddlers, you may see three different types of emerging musical play with instruments or materials that make sounds: dramatic play, scientific play, and musical play.

Dramatic Play. Children who have seen a concert in the media or attended one in person may do a dramatic play. Children will pretend to play the instrument, impersonating a musician or a character they know who plays a musical instrument. If a child stands up holding two plastic spoons from the pretend area and swings in curly motions as if pretending to be a maestro while listening to classical music in the background, that action could be dramatic play.

Scientific Play. Those children who are interested in investigating or messing about with the sound materials or musical instruments to make different kinds of sounds, such as Steve at the swimming pool or Martin and Jalen at the beginning of this chapter, are engaging in scientific play, which is the focus of this chapter. This type of play helps children foster critical thinking skills and develop creative confidence.

Musical Play. Educators also may have children who enjoy musical play and try playing a song or jamming with other children. This may be more in evidence with older children. For toddlers who are still capable of hearing various frequencies of sound, we suggest providing experiences that enrich their scientific knowledge and allow them to be explorers, investigators, and discoverers of sound.

Textbox 9.5. Amal Explores Tin Can Sounds

Amal arranged multiple tin cans of different sizes and placed them upside-down. She made sure that the cans were lined up next to one another. Holding a metal spoon facing upward, Amal struck the top of each can from right to left, tapping the first three cans twice, then tapping eight times on the smaller fourth can. She then looked somewhat pensively to the side as she appeared to notice that this fourth can produced a lower sound. Then Amal struck the last can twice again. As if her drumming performance were over, she stopped with her spoon elevated in the air, stepped back, smiled, mumbled, and then stepped forward to tap each can gently with her fingers, this time from left to right. During the process, Amal seemed to be singing or verbalizing something, as if she was counting or speaking to the cans. Her eyes were completely focused on her musical project. She then held the spoon with her right hand again and struck the cans from left to right, as she did with her fingers. At the end, she held the spoon in the air, as if signaling the end of her performance.

These 33 seconds of Amal's scientific exploration and performance were intense and focused, without any intervention by the educators, who sat close by on the floor, facing her, but reading books to other children. When children are deeply engaged with materials of their preference, being autonomous is the first step for independent thinking and problem solving. Amal paused at her scientific problem—the fourth can—but she decided to move on with her exploration, not letting it interfere with the process. Amal was satisfied with her original collection of percussion instruments and her skill in playing them, so the sound was pleasing to her. She was aware of the presence of the educators in the area, but preferred to stay engaged with her sound exploration, requiring no adult intervention. Her exploration may have appeared to be dramatic play until the observer noticed the details of her inquiry-based actions and saw her thinking process. Because the educators had chosen to videotape this performance, they had the opportunity to watch Amal several times in order to see the full measure of her investigation. Providing this safe environment with lots of opportunities for children to explore, investigate, and find the solutions to their problems, no matter how small they are, creates a rich learning opportunity where children can thrive.

ITM: Engaging Older Toddlers. Sound exploration with older toddlers is an inquiry-based activity focused on the phenomena that can be producible, immediate, perceptible, and variable (Kamii & DeVries, 1993), as described in the beginning of this book. Exploring sound is a unique and important science activity using ears and hearing instead of eyes to learn and increase knowledge, and educators should be sure to distinguish it from a passive listening activity, music and movement, or a sensory activity. Sound exploration is an engaging activity in which children can make discoveries about sound and become aware of similarities and differences in sounds, which allows them to focus on cause-and-effect relationships. With verbal toddlers, using open-ended questions or productive questions (Elstgeest, 1985) can engage them in challenges that may require critical thinking skills and perseverance. For example, young children often confuse high and low pitches or frequency. The high pitch of a smoke alarm easily can be confused with loudness. A high pitch also can be confused with something that is tall (e.g., skyscraper), especially if you use hand gestures to define what is high and what is low pitch. A good use of open-ended questions such as, "How can you make the pitch lower with your voice?" or "What would happen if . . . ," may help children to stay focused or reflect on the experience. Learning to differentiate the components of sound, such as pitch and loudness, is a long-term process, requiring direct instruction and modeling, and multiple opportunities for individual experience. Offering opportunities to strengthen the experience through sound exploration becomes an important learning goal achieved only through children's engagement with intentional materials with adults or more experienced peers who can guide and scaffold their understanding.

ITM: Providing Opportunities. The vignette with Steve, who explored sound in the swimming pool, also could occur with older toddlers. In the multiple possibilities available for exploration in the classroom, children may engage in building structures with blocks and suddenly find themselves tapping two blocks together because they heard a friend across the room who was drumming.

TEXTBOX 9.6. SERVE-AND-RETURN RHYTHM

We observed Maria, who was playing at the construction table, hammering a peg with a plastic hammer. She had a rhythmical way to hammer the peg, making a pattern of hammering three times, then a pause, then three times again. Jack was painting while Maria was hammering, and he began to add three dots to his watercolor masterpiece, while he softly mumbled, "cha-cha-cha…cha-cha-cha," synchronizing with Maria's peg work. They did not look at each other or even speak to each other. However, their teacher could see the connection and the magical call-and-response moment between these two toddlers, who were completely focused on their own activities.

Opportunities also can be presented intentionally, if the educators are aware that their children may need a different challenge. Offering an original string-based instrument such as a tin can with a stretched rubber band on the opened end of the can, or a milk or juice container guitar (see Figure 9.11), may trigger their curiosity, especially if they can hear different pitches caused by the tension of the rubber band. If you relax the rubber band, you will

Figure 9.11. Milk Carton Guitar

have a lower sound. Stretch it, and you will have a higher sound. Would it have the same effect if you switch the can to, let's say, a glass jar? How different would it be? This exploration must be supervised closely due to safety issues, but it is a fascinating opportunity for children to expand their understanding of sound, and the quality of sound produced by different variables that amplify the sound.

ITM: Making Decisions. Documenting children's explorations with sound would be ideal if it was accompanied by a video-recording device. By making children's sound exploration visual, educators will be able to revisit the same scenario many times and find out what children are thinking. The clues found in children's facial and body expressions, in the way they hold the materials, and in the pauses and puzzled faces they may make in between their explorations provide rich information about children's learning. If video recording is not a possibility, we suggest taking pictures, lowering the camera lens to the children's eye level or focusing only on their hands when working on the materials. By taking the pictures from this lower position, or from the same level as children's engagement, you will find rich details that will help with documentation and making fruitful decisions for your children.

EDUCATOR PLANNING FOR SOUND

We understand the difficulty when making decisions about purchasing materials for your classroom so that children have high-quality opportunities for inquiry learning. You may find a wonderful collection of materials in the school supply catalog you receive in your mailbox periodically, but your school budget does not allow for this kind of expense. Before this creates an additional stress on your very busy day of planning, we suggest you look for materials that can be found anywhere, and at an affordable price. Visit a discount store or resale shop with your educator lens and think about sound and how it can be explored safely. Walk through every aisle thinking, "What kind of sound would this make?" "How would I classify this material as a type of instrument?" "How could I combine this material with another?" This is one of our favorite shopping excursions, and our attics and basements can prove it! When you are completely focused on sound materials and the challenges you can offer to the children, you will be amazed at what you can find. To facilitate your thoughts, we introduced you to a comprehensive table (see Figure 9.9), indicating the classification of musical instruments, examples of some musical instruments in the category, and affordable or homemade materials or tools that fit into the same category. Which instrument would make children think and be engaged? Which problems would they attempt to solve?

The examples of "affordable instruments or materials" are just a few of the materials that can be found at stores, among recyclables, or at a garage sale in your neighborhood. Notice that there are only five classifications of musical instruments (Midgley, 1976), although there are thousands of creative instruments that fit under these classifications. When you select the materials or think about offering an engaging opportunity to young children, think about these classifications as a useful reference. Of the five, the electrical instrument is the least appropriate for very young children, as most instruments that produce sound electronically do not offer opportunities for children to learn through inquiry. For example, an electronic piano does not show how sounds differ from one another, while a chordophone piano can demonstrate visually how strings of different sizes and lengths function to produce a sound. It is unfortunate that the most popular sound materials found in children's toys are of electronic origin. We suggest a hands-on material and minds-on inquiry activity for young children's sound exploration.

Sounds are all around us. Many we do not notice at all. Others invade our consciousness in both good and troubling ways. And each of us has preferences for particular sounds. Educators can introduce and encourage sound explorations with very young children that will support memory development, curiosity, and open enjoyment of sounds and music from a wide variety of cultures and genres. In addition, experiences like the ones described in this chapter will lay a foundation for later school explorations, experiences, and understandings about how sounds are made and varied.

Afterword

Sherri Peterson and Jill Uhlenberg

Our purpose in writing this book has been twofold—to describe our view of inquiry learning and teaching with children from birth to 3 and to provide a resource for rich classroom experiences that will engage children's active minds. It is our hope that this book has been written for you, an early childhood educator and teacher researcher. In our work, we see educators who slip into the role of teacher researcher when they begin to examine their beliefs about learning and teaching. We have all been there! We came from very different places before our work brought us together. As we began to think about learning and teaching differently, we supported one another. This shift in thinking about our work with children was difficult. As a mentor once said to one of us, "When we know better, we do better." So we applaud you if you are ready to explore inquiry learning and teaching, and we urge you to find a "thinking partner" who shares your passion for lifelong learning.

THE INQUIRY TEACHING MODEL

As you support infants and toddlers who are learning about the world around them, we invite you to investigate the inquiry teaching model. Observe closely to find the deeper meaning in what infants and toddlers are doing. Record what is happening in the classroom in order to plan for children's learning. Use your observations to spark conversations with your teaching partners and with families to reveal children's interests. Share the stories that emerge from your observations so that the learning becomes visible to children and families on the walls and in the halls. "When we put inquiry at the heart of our programs, we organize our curriculum for children and for teachers around observation, study, and responsive planning" (Pelo, 2006, p. 53).

Your observations will guide you to prepare the environment, choose materials, and plan experiences that will engage the young learners in your classroom. As you explore inquiry teaching, these infants and toddlers will have the opportunity to engage in inquiry learning. They will wonder about and explore the materials that are offered and begin to use old strategies and develop new ones to solve the unique problems that they pose for themselves. Their determination to find solutions to these problems will fuel their wonder and continue the inquiry cycle as they become actively engaged in their learning. Investigations with open-ended materials can be messy, but we urge you to look beyond the muddle to find the meaning in children's actions with materials that you have prepared thoughtfully based on children's interests. Your intentional efforts will provide opportunities for every child in your care, no matter their abilities, language, or culture.

A TALE OF IMPERFECTION

We have been working toward inquiry learning and teaching for many years, and we are not finished yet. Nor has our journey been without bumps. We have made many missteps along the way. Our work with sound is an example.

Years ago, we decided we wanted to offer materials so that toddlers could explore sounds. We thought the best materials would be those that were familiar to them, so we developed a kitchen band. From the first day, we learned a great deal about both the materials and the toddlers.

We collected a variety of pots and pans, along with some safe kitchen utensils to use to strike the pans. Staff started by placing the pans upside-down to offer the pan bottoms as the place to hit. After discussions, we began to discourage adults from this practice so that the children could choose to position the pans and thus note a difference between striking the pan inside or outside on the bottom.

This made no difference to the toddlers, who were excited to be able to beat the pans loudly with full power. The noise was deafening, but we hoped that the children eventually would settle down and explore. That didn't happen. Some toddlers eventually became saturated with the noise and left the area to find other, quieter activities. Adults also left the area to avoid the noise.

On the following days, fewer and fewer toddlers came to the kitchen band center until only one or two came for a short time, beating pans enthusiastically and then wandering away. Their actions were loud but brief. There was nothing to keep their interest level high. Eventually the pans and utensils became pretend play materials, and the kitchen band became just a kitchen.

Our conversations about these events led us to dramatically change the materials. We became more thoughtful about what kinds of sounds we wanted to explore and what materials would be needed. We wondered what would attract the toddlers, strategized how to engage them and keep their attention, and wondered what kinds of problems they would find to solve. In other words, we used an inquiry approach to improve our teaching. And it took us a long time to come to the ideas we presented in Chapter 9 on sound.

The moral of our story is to be kind to yourself as you use an inquiry approach to your teaching. Nobody does it perfectly at first. Try things, strategize, analyze your success, and then figure out how to improve. The missteps you take are often more important than the successes.

We have been working with young children and their educators for over 4 decades, and we continue to learn about infant and toddler learning and teaching each time we observe in a classroom, watch a videotaped classroom experience, or (for some of us) analyze our interactions with our own grandchildren—which we can't help but do! For some educators, the idea of observing, documenting, and reflecting on children's actions might be a new way of thinking about their role in an infant or toddler environment. And the idea that there is time in a busy day filled with caregiving tasks is an even bigger stretch. But we urge you to give inquiry learning and teaching a try. The rewards will be worth the effort. The infants and toddlers you are sharing your days with deserve this careful attention to their learning. You deserve to see yourself as a professional who is a capable learner and caring educator.

Share these ideas with your administrator and let your team help you to prioritize the experiences you might use to introduce the materials with the space you have available. Ask your administrator to help you find time to collaborate with your team and plan for new experiences for the infants and toddlers. Find additional resources to help you in your journey. We have included a list of materials in each chapter and a reference list to help you get started. We have a website (https://regentsctr.uni.edu/) with additional resources, and we invite you to visit the pages designed especially for infant and toddler educators.

We will continue to do our own research and use what we learn to update the website. We also urge you to contact us with questions, photos of your work, and comments about what works and what needs further consideration. We, too, have plans to try some new things with the infants and toddlers we see regularly. Next on our list are more water investigations, some work with loose parts, and ideas for finding the STEM in everyday activities. We also want to do more thinking and learning about developing a community of practice with infant and toddler educators so that they have opportunities to share their thinking about children's thinking in a quest to embrace the joy of teaching children in this age group.

References

Armstrong, K. (2019, April 30). How sound becomes music. *Association for Psychological Science.* https://www.psychologicalscience.org/observer/how-sound-becomes-music

Bell, R. (2017). Watching the babies: The why, what, and how of observation as assessment in infant and toddler care. *Dimensions of Early Childhood, 45*(1), 4–10.

Boston Children's Museum. (2013). Brain building for STEM. *STEM sprouts: Science, technology, engineering & math teaching guide.* https://bostonchildrensmuseum.org/sites/default/files/pdfs/STEMGuide.pdf

Carr, M., & Lee, W. (2012). *Learning stories: Constructing learner identities in early education.* SAGE.

Carr, M., & Lee, W. (2019). *Learning stories in practice.* SAGE.

Center for Applied Special Technology. (2018). *UDL and the learning brain.* https://udlguidelines.cast.org/

Center on the Developing Child, Harvard University. (2007). *The science of early childhood development: Closing the gap between what we know and what we do.* https://developingchild.harvard.edu/resources/the-science-of-early-childhood-development-closing-the-gap-between-what-we-know-and-what-we-do/

Center on the Developing Child, Harvard University. (2011). *Building the brain's "air traffic control" system: How early experiences shape the development of executive function* (Working Paper No. 11).

Center on the Developing Child, Harvard University. (2021). *A guide to serve and return: How your interaction with children can build brains.* https://devhcdc.wpengine.com/guide/a-guide-to-serve-and-return-how-your-interaction-with-children-can-build-brains/

Chalufour, I., & Worth, K. (2004). *Building structures with young children.* Redleaf Press.

Chen, Z., Siegler, R. S., & Daehler, M. W. (2000). Across the great divide: Bridging the gap between understanding of toddlers' and older children's thinking. *Monographs of the Society for Research in Child Development, 65*(2). http://www.jstor.org/stable/3181574

Clements, D., & Sarama, J. (2009). *Learning and teaching early math: The learning trajectories approach.* Routledge.

Counsell, S., Escalada, L., Geiken, R., Sander, M., Uhlenberg, J., Van Meeteren, B., Yoshizawa, S., & Zan, B. (2016). *STEM learning with young children: Inquiry teaching with ramps and pathways.* Teachers College Press.

Curtis, D. (2017). *Really seeing children: A collection of teaching and learning stories.* Exchange Press.

Dombro, A. L., Jablon, J. R., & Stetson, C. (2011). *Powerful interactions: How to connect with children to extend their learning.* National Association for the Education of Young Children.

Drummond, T. (2017). *Connecting to children.* https://tomdrummond.com/helping-other-adults/connecting-to-children/

Duncan, S., Martin, J., & Haughey, S. (2018). *Through a child's eyes: How classroom design inspires learning and wonder.* Gryphon House.

Elstgeest, J. (1985). The right question at the right time. In W. Harlen (Ed.), *Primary science: Taking the plunge* (pp. 36–46). Heinemann Educational.

Foreman, G., & Hall, E. (2005). Wondering with children: The importance of observations in early education. *Early Childhood Research and Practice, 7*(2). https://ecrp.illinois.edu/v7n2/forman.html

Francis, K., & Whitely, W. (2015). Interactions between three dimensions and two dimensions. In B. Davis & Spatial Reasoning Study Group (Eds.), *Spatial reasoning in the early years: Principles, assertions, and speculations* (pp. 121–136). Routledge.

Gandini, L. (1998). Educational and caring spaces. In C. Edwards, L. Gandini, & G. Foreman (Eds.), *The hundred languages of children: The Reggio Emilia approach—Advanced reflections* (2nd ed., pp. 161–178). Ablex.

Geiken, R. (2011). *Cylinders and spheres: Toddlers engage in problem solving* [Doctoral dissertation, University of Northern Iowa]. Electronic Theses and Dissertations, 442. https://scholarworks.uni.edu/etd/442

Gopnik, A. (2010). How babies think. *Scientific American, 303*(1), 76–81.

Greenfield, D. B., Alexander, A., & Frechette, E. (2017). Unleashing the power of science in early childhood: A foundation for high-quality interactions and learning. *Zero to Three, 37*(5), 13–21.

Greenman, J. (2007). *Caring spaces, learning places: Environments that work*. Exchange Press.

Gros-Louis, J., West, M. J., & King, A. P. (2014). Maternal responsiveness and the development of directed vocalizing in social interactions. *Infancy, 19*(4), 385–408. https://doi.org/10.1111/infa.12054

Hamlin, M., & Wisneski, D. (2012). Supporting the scientific thinking and inquiry of toddlers and preschoolers through play. *Young Children, 67*(3), 82–88.

Hawkins, D. (1965). Messing about in science. *Science and Children, 2*(5), 5–9.

Heroman, C., Burts, D. C., Berke, K., & Bickart, T. S. (2010). *The creative curriculum for preschool: Vol. 5. Objectives for development & learning: Birth through kindergarten*. Teaching Strategies.

HighScope Educational Research Foundation. (2015). *Infant-toddler COR advantage*. HighScope Press.

Hildebrandt, C., & Zan, B. (2002). Exploring the art and science of musical sounds. In R. DeVries, B. Zan, C. Hildebrandt, R. Edmiaston, & C. Sales, *Developing constructivist early childhood curriculum* (p. 101–119). Teachers College Press.

Hoisington, C., Chalufour, I., Winokur, J., & Clark-Chiarelli, N. (2014). Promoting children's science inquiry and learning through water investigations. *Young Children, 69*(4), 72–79.

Iowa Department of Education. (2018). *Iowa early learning standards* (3rd ed.). https://educateiowa.gov/documents/early-childhood-standards/2019/01/iowa-early-learning-standards-3rd-edition

Jablon, J., Dombro, A., & Dichtelmiller, M. (2007). *The power of observation: Birth to age 8* (2nd ed.). Teaching Strategies.

Johnson, H. (1996). *The art of blockbuilding*. National Association for the Education of Young Children. (Original work published 1933)

Kamii, C., & DeVries, R. (1993). *Physical knowledge in preschool education: Implications of Piaget's theory*. Teachers College Press. (Original work published 1978)

Kamii, C., Miyakawa, Y., & Kato, Y. (2004). The development of logico-mathematical knowledge in the block-building activity at ages 1–4. *Journal of Research in Childhood Education, 19*, 44–57.

Knauf, H. (2019). Physical environments of early childhood education centres: Facilitating and inhibiting factors supporting children's participation. *International Journal of Early Childhood, 51*, 355–372. https://doi.org/10.1007/s13158-019-00254-3

Kraus, N., & Slater, J. (2015). Music and language: Relations and disconnections. *Handbook of clinical neurology, 129*(3), 207–222.

Kuhl, P. K. (2010a). Brain mechanisms in early language acquisition. *Neuron, 67*(5), 713–727. https://doi.org/10.1016/j.neuron.2010.08.038

Kuhl, P. K. (2010b, October). *The linguistic genius of babies* [Video]. https://www.ted.com/talks/patricia_kuhl_the_linguistic_genius_of_babies?language=en.

Lally, J. R. (2005). *Infants have their own curriculum: A responsive approach to curriculum planning for infants and toddlers*. Community Playthings. https://www.communityplaythings.com/resources/articles/2005/Infants-Have-Their-Own-Curriculum

Lally, J. R. (2009). The science and psychology of infant and toddler care: How an understanding of early learning has transformed child care. *ZERO to THREE, 30*(2), 47–53.

Lally, J. R., & Mangione, P. (2017). Caring relationships: The heart of early brain development. *Young Children, 72*(2), 17–24.

Lewin-Benham, A. (2010). *Infants and toddlers at work: Using Reggio-inspired materials to support brain development*. Teachers College Press.

Martens, M. L. (1999). Productive questions: Tools for supporting constructivist learning. *Science and Children, 36*, 24–27.

McClure, E. (2017). More than a foundation: Young children are capable STEM learners. *Young Children, 72*(5), 83–89.

McClure, E. R., Guernsey, L., Clements, D. H., Bales, S. N., Nichols, J., Kendall-Taylor, N., & Levine, M. (2017). *STEM starts early: Grounding science, technology, engineering, and math education in early childhood*. The Joan Ganz Cooney Center at Sesame Workshop.

Mehegan, L., & Rainville, G. (2020, June). *Music nourishes and delights: 2020 music and brain health survey*. AARP Research. https://doi.org/10.26419/res.00387.001

Midgley, R. (1976). *Musical instruments of the world: An illustrated encyclopedia with more than 4000 original drawings*. Facts on File.

Merriam-Webster. (n.d.). Inquiry. In *Merriam-Webster.com dictionary*. https://merriam-webster.com/dictionary/inquiry

National Association for the Education of Young Children. (2014). *NSTA position statement: Early childhood science education*. https://www.naeyc.org/sites/default/files/globally-shared/downloads/PDFs/resources/position-statements/Early%20Childhood%20FINAL%20FINAL%201-30-14%20%281%29%20%281%29.pdf

National Association for the Education of Young Children. (2019). *Advancing equity in early childhood education position statement*. https://www.naeyc.org/resources/position-statements/equity

National Association for the Education of Young Children. (2020). *Developmentally appropriate practice: National*

Association for the Education of Young Children (Position Statement). https://www.naeyc.org/sites/default/files/globally-shared/downloads/PDFs/resources/position-statements/dap-statement_0.pdf

National Research Council. (2001). *Eager to learn: Educating our preschoolers*. National Academies Press. https://doi.org/10.17226/9745

National Science Teachers Association. (2014). *NSTA position statement: Early childhood science education*. https://www.naeyc.org/sites/default/files/globally-shared/downloads/PDFs/resources/position-statements/Early%20Childhood%20FINAL%20FINAL%201-30-14%20%281%29%20%281%29.pdf

National Scientific Council on the Developing Child. (2004). *Children's emotional development is built into the architecture of their brains* (Working Paper No. 2). https://developingchild.harvard.edu/resources/childrens-emotional-development-is-built-into-the-architecture-of-their-brains/

Pelo, A. (2006, November/December). Growing a culture of inquiry: Observation as professional development. *Exchange*, 50–53. http://www.childcareexchange.com/article/growing-a-culture-of-inquiry-observation-as-professional-development/5017250/

Piaget, J. (1954). *The construction of reality in the child* (M. Cook, Trans.). Basic Books.

Piaget, J., & Inhelder, B. (1967). *The child's conception of space*. Norton.

Post, J., Hohmann, M., & Epstein, A. S. (2011). *Tender care and early learning: Supporting infants and toddlers in child care settings* (2nd ed.). HighScope Press https://highscope.org/product/tender-care-and-early-learning-2nd-ed/

Pruden, S. M., Levine, S. C., & Huttenlocher, J. (2011). Children's spatial thinking: Does talk about the spatial world matter? *Developmental Science, 14*(6), 1417–1430. https://doi.org/10.1111/j.1467-7687.2011.01088.x

Rinaldi, C. (1994). Staff development in Reggio Emilia. In L. Katz & B. Cesarone (Eds.), *Reflections on the Reggio Emilia approach*. ERIC Clearinghouse on Elementary and Early Childhood Education.

Salmon, A., & Barrera, M. (2021). What are you thinking? Scaffolding thinking to promote learning. *Young Children, 76*(2), 58–63.

Spaepen, E., Bowman, B., Day, C. B., Chen, J., Cunningham, C., Donohue, C., Espinosa, L., Gartzman, M., Greenfield, D., Leslie, D., Levine, S., McCray, J., Schauble, L., & Worth, K. (2017). *Early STEM matters: Providing high-quality STEM experiences for all young learners*. Early Childhood STEM Working Group. https://ecstem.uchicago.edu/

Stacey, S. (2019). *Inquiry-based early learning environments: Creating, supporting, and collaborating*. Redleaf Press.

Uhlenberg, J., & Geiken, R. (2020). Supporting young children's spatial understanding: Examining toddlers' experiences with contents and containers. *Early Childhood Education Journal*. https://doi.org/10.1007/s10643-020-01050-8

U.S. Department of Health and Human Services, Administration on Children, Youth and Families/Office of Head Start. (2015). *Head Start early learning outcomes framework: Ages birth to five*. https://eclkc.ohs.acf.hhs.gov/interactive-head-start-early-learning-outcomes-framework-ages-birth-five

Warden, C. (2021). *Inquiries: A guide to planning with and for children, Issue 1*. Mindstretchers Academy. https://us.mindstretchers.academy/shop/free-download-inquiries-issue-1-what-is-inquiry-based-learning

Wien, C. (2014). *The power of emergent curriculum: Stories from early childhood classrooms*. National Association for the Education of Young Children.

Wittmer, D. S., & Petersen, S. H. (2018). *Infant and toddler development and responsive program planning: A relationship-based approach* (4th ed.). Pearson.

Worth, K. (2010). Science in early childhood classrooms: Content and process. *Early Childhood Research & Practice, 12*(2). http://ecrp.illinois.edu/beyond/seed/worth.html

Index

The letter *f* following a page number indicates a figure.

2D versus 3D objects and spatial understanding, 59

About the Contributors

Beth Dykstra Van Meeteren is director of the Iowa Regents' Center for Early Developmental Education at the University of Northern Iowa. Her areas of research include early STEM, early engineering, and integrative STEM and literacy.

Rosemary Geiken is a retired associate professor of early childhood. Her work with infants and toddlers focuses on STEM experiences and problem solving as well as professional development for infant/toddler educators.

Sherri Peterson is the program coordinator at the Iowa Regents' Center for Early Developmental Education. She has worked as an early childhood special education teacher, Early ACCESS coordinator, consultant, coach, and adult educator for over 4 decades in both rural and urban settings. She is an advocate for equitable learning environments for all children.

Jill Uhlenberg is an emerita associate professor of early childhood education. Her primary foci have been on infant and toddler learning, problem solving, and curriculum development, and their relationship to teacher education.

Sonia Yoshizawa is the coordinator of research and services at the East Tennessee State University Center of Excellence in Early Childhood Learning and Development. She has worked as a lead teacher, director, speaker, and consultant. Her focus is early childhood STEM, music, and professional development with infant/toddler educators.